The MindRight Legacy Builders Program

Abundance is Your Birthright!

by

ASH'CASH

DISCLAIMER

The advice contained in this material might not be suitable for everyone. The author designed the information to present his opinion about the subject matter. The reader must carefully investigate all aspects of any business decision before committing him or herself. The author obtained the information contained herein from sources he believes to be reliable and from his own personal experience, but he neither implies nor intends any guarantee of accuracy. The author is not in the business of giving legal, accounting, or any other type of professional advice. Should the reader need such advice, he or she must seek services from a competent professional. The author particularly disclaims any liability, loss, or risk taken by individuals who directly or indirectly act on the information contained herein. The author believes the advice presented here is sound, but readers cannot hold him responsible for either the actions they take or the risk taken by individuals who directly or indirectly act on the information contained herein.

Published by 1BrickPublishing

A division of Ash Cash Enterprises, LLC

Printed in the United States

ISBN 978-1-949303-12-4

MINDRIGHT
MONEY MANAGEMENT

Table of Contents

Welcome - Redefining Financial Freedom

The term financial freedom has been thrown around so much that people are starting to believe that there is this one way to become financially free.

The truth of the matter is, financial freedom is whatever you say it is. It is the act of being free from worrying about money and the act of being able to use your time and money, however you want to use it.

You must understand that there needs to be a shift in the relationship you have with money. If you are exchanging time for money, then it is impossible for you to be financially free.

Money needs to work for you! The goal is to create a system in which you are not physically working for money. If you do not come from money, then you may have to actively work for money at first, but ultimately your goal should be to not have to continue to exchange your time for money.

This is not to say that the things that you do with your time can't produce money, but money should not be the ultimate goal. In fact, ideally what you do with your time should be something that you absolutely love and as a result money will be a byproduct...

In the classic book, Think and Grow Rich by Napoleon Hill, he discusses what "true" riches are. His list of 12 "true" riches includes:

1. A Positive Mental Attitude (observe that it heads the list!)
2. Sound Physical Health
3. Harmony in Human Relations
4. Freedom from Fear
5. The Hope of Future Achievement
6. The Capacity for Applied Faith
7. Willingness to Share One's Blessings with Others
8. To Be Engaged in a Labor of Love
9. An Open Mind on All Subjects Toward All People
10. Complete Self-Discipline
11. Wisdom with Which to Understand People
12. Financial Security

Financial security is last because all of the other riches generate money aka financial security.

Another example of someone who had a good perspective on how to build financial freedom and prosperity is the late Frederick J. Eikerenkoetter II. better known as Reverend Ike. Reverend Ike. was an African- American Minister and Evangelist based in New York City.

Known for the slogan "You can't lose with the stuff I use!" His preaching is considered a form of prosperity theology. but in essence. he uses the bible and the word of God to prove that abundance is your birthright. His order of riches are: Good health + Happiness + Love Success + Prosperity + Money!

Notice. once again money is last on the list. The reason why I am emphasizing this is because in your quest for financial freedom I do not want you to believe that if you focus on money it will create the outcome that you want. It is actually the opposite. As you focus on your health. happiness. and do everything with love. then success. prosperity and money WILL be yours!

This workbook consists of 12 activities that you MUST follow and complete if you are looking for true financial freedom. Please take a moment to print this book out. (if you are viewing the digital version) and be thoughtful about your answers. There's power in writing things down so it is important that you are putting pen (or pencil) to paper.

One Last Note:

Obtaining success in anything is an exact science. There are four steps and they include:

1. Deciding what you want
2. Believing that it's possible and that you deserve it.
3. Focusing on it and visualizing it as if it's already yours
4. Paying the price by being disciplined. putting in the effort and persevering. despite any external circumstances.

This is important to note. because while most of this book will be practical things that you need to do in order to get your finances in order. "Paying the price" also includes the "mindset" work that MUST happen in order for the "practical things" to work. Keep this in mind as you complete each activity in the workbook

Meet Your Mindright Money Coach

Ash Cash Exantus is one of the nation's top financial educators. He is a personal finance expert, motivational speaker, and the author of many books, including four Amazon.com bestsellers.

Dubbed as the Financial Motivator, he uses a culturally responsive approach in teaching financial literacy, wealth building and entrepreneurship.

He is the founder and Chief Financial Educator at MindRight Money Management, a Financial Education and Media company that blends psychology and personal finance to help people manage their money better in order to live the life that they want.

He is the host of The Ash Cash Show, a daily business and finance news show that focuses on personal finance and empowering people to achieve financial freedom and build wealth.

Above all of his credentials, accolades, and titles, ***Ash is simply known for helping people maximize their full potential.*** For more information about Ash Please visit

www.IamAshCash.com

Your Financial Freedom Checklist/Declaration

Below you will find your financial freedom checklist. It is also your declaration of your new life. Read each of them out loud and vibrate on the wave of every word that is being said. At the end please sign your name and commit to living by these declarations.

I NOW DECLARE THAT...

...I am committed to change. Going forward I ONLY act in a responsible manner with my finances. I understand that money is a tool to help build a better now and future and I am declaring that I will use this tool the right way.

...In order for me to get what I want out of life, I must decide exactly what it is that I want. I am declaring that going forward, I will ask for and declare EXACTLY what I want out of life without limiting myself or the universe.

...I know that life and death is in the power of the tongue and what I say and feel will become my reality. I now declare that I am changing my money language. Everything in abundance and I deserve and expect MORE than enough.

...I know that emergencies are things that we are not prepared for. I declare to always have six to eight months of expenses in an account so I am prepared for any storms that may come. I will no longer call this account my "emergency account" since "emergencies" are not the experiences that I am preparing for. I now call my savings account, my "Financial Freedom Fund and look forward to achieving this status very soon.

...The power of visualization is real. I will only use my imagination, for visualizing the life that I want. I will no longer waste time on worry, which is using my imagination for things that I don't want.

...I understand that in order to live my best life I must not work for money, but instead money needs to work for me. I now declare that I will diversify my income by creating multiple streams and begin to invest my money into income producing assets. My goal is to no longer exchange time for money and instead will get paid for the value that I bring.

...I know that debt can be a gift or a curse depending on how I use it. I now declare to eliminate bad debt, but will also not look at debt as the enemy. I understand that if used the right way, debt can be a powerful wealth-building tool. I declare to only use debt in this way.

...I understand the power of the mastermind and know that in order to go far I must go together with a like-minded tribe. I vow to create my money accountability team to make sure that wealth and abundance is the only language that I understand, and I will move with my team who helped me get there.

...I will continue to build wealth, not just for me, but for my family and community. I will use the proper tools to acquire asset protection, to make sure that my legacy, and those that come behind me, will be secured. I now declare financial freedom and generational wealth for life, and beyond.

(Signature) X____________________________

(Print Name) X____________________________

(Date) ____________________________

Defining Your Current Money Story

Today begins the day that you start working towards building the financial abundance that is already reserved for you. In order to get you to your next level financially, we must know where you are right now. It is my intention with this program to give you a step-by-step plan on how to live your best financial life. More specifically, we want to help those who want to become millionaires, get there as quickly as possible using the personal, intellectual, social and financial capital that is already in their possession.

The following questions will help us craft a plan that is specific to your needs.

What are the ten most important things that you want to accomplish while you're on this Earth?

1. ______________________________

2. ______________________________

3. ______________________________

MINDRIGHT
MONEY MANAGEMENT

4.

5.

6.

7.

8.

9.

10.

MINDRIGHT
MONEY MANAGEMENT

If money were no object, what would you be doing right now?

What is your current net worth? (What you OWN minus What you OWE) IE: My house is Worth $800,000 and I owe a $200,000 mortgage so my net worth is $600,000

- ❑ I have a negative Net Worth
- ❑ $0-$100,000
- ❑ $100,000 - $500,000
- ❑ $500,000 - $1MM
- ❑ Over $1MM

MILLIONAIRE MINDSET

Do you want to be a millionaire?

- ❑ Yes
- ❑ No
- ❑ Not Sure

Do you think it is possible for you?

- ❑ Yes
- ❑ No
- ❑ Not Sure

Would you be the 1st millionaire in your family?

- ❑ Yes
- ❑ No
- ❑ Not Sure

Do you personally know any millionaires right now (as in you can call them on the phone)?

- ❑ Yes
- ❑ No
- ❑ Not Sure

Do you have a written plan to become a millionaire?

- ❑ Yes
- ❑ No
- ❑ Not Sure

What would being a millionaire mean for/to you?

How many years do you think it will take you to become a millionaire doing what you're doing now and why?

In one sentence, describe your wealth-building strategy besides "Make more money?" What do you think is your path to becoming a millionaire?

What is slowing down or stopping you from becoming a millionaire faster?

What are the top ways you make money today?

- ❑ My 9-5
- ❑ 2nd job (e.g. Uber)
- ❑ A side hustle (part-time entrepreneurship)
- ❑ Full-time entrepreneurship (product)
- ❑ Full-time entrepreneurship (service)
- ❑ Silent partner/Investor in a business
- ❑ Franchise owner
- ❑ Real estate investing (e.g. rental income, AirBnB)
- ❑ Stock market investing, Day trading, and/or Cryptocurrency

What do you want the top 1-2 ways you make money to be in 5-10 years?

- ❑ My 9-5
- ❑ 2nd job (e.g. Uber)
- ❑ A side hustle (part-time entrepreneurship)
- ❑ Full-time entrepreneurship (product)
- ❑ Full-time entrepreneurship (service)
- ❑ Silent partner/Investor in a business
- ❑ Franchise owner
- ❑ Real estate investing (e.g. rental income, AirBnB)
- ❑ Stock market investing, Day trading, and/or Cryptocurrency

What liabilities (debt) are you trying to pay off right now?

- ❑ I don't have any debt
- ❑ Student loans
- ❑ Credit card debt
- ❑ Car note / loan
- ❑ Mortgage
- ❑ Taxes
- ❑ Business loan
- ❑ I owe my family money

How much is your total debt obligation?

- ❑ I don't owe anyone ANYTHING!
- ❑ $0 - $50,000
- ❑ $50,000 - $100,000

- ❑ $100,000 - $500,000
- ❑ $500,000 - $1MM
- ❑ I went absolutely crazy with debt

What are the top 2 assets you are investing in right now?

- ❑ Myself & mindset
- ❑ Savings account
- ❑ My career advancement
- ❑ Formal education
- ❑ Certifications (with the hopes of more income)
- ❑ Stocks, Bonds, Mutual Funds and/or Crypto
- ❑ Retirement accounts (401K, IRA, etc)
- ❑ My own business
- ❑ Real estate (Buy and Hold)
- ❑ Silent Investor/Partner in Someone else' business

What best describes your Entrepreneurial status right now?

- ❑ I want to be my own boss but have no clue on where to start
- ❑ I have lots of ideas, but can't choose which I should run with first
- ❑ I have an idea, but having trouble getting started
- ❑ I usually start an idea, then stop. Start again, then stop.
- ❑ I'm currently making $1,000-$4,000/month in revenue
- ❑ I'm currently making $4,000-$8,000/month in revenue
- ❑ I'm currently making $100,000+/year in revenue

What best describes your living situation right now?

- ❑ I am currently living at home
- ❑ I am renting an apartment/home
- ❑ I bought a single-family home
- ❑ I invested in a multi-family home that I currently live in
- ❑ I bought a home and have investment property as well

How much would you have to earn per year 5 years from now to be happy?

- ❑ $0 - $50,000
- ❑ $50,000 - $100,000
- ❑ $100,000 - $500,000
- ❑ $500,000 - $1MM
- ❑ $1MM+

How much money would you like to have in your bank account by next year?

- ❑ $0 - $50,000
- ❑ $50,000 - $100,000
- ❑ $100,000 - $500,000
- ❑ $500,000 - $1MM
- ❑ $1MM+

How much money would you like to have in your bank account in 5 years?

- ❑ $0 - $50,000
- ❑ $50,000 - $100,000
- ❑ $100,000 - $500,000
- ❑ $500,000 - $1MM
- ❑ $1MM+

What will your life look like once you reach your financial goals? (e.g. What kind of house will you have? What car do you drive? How often do you vacation?) No restrictions! Dream BIG!

Dream life (cont'd)

How do you manage & monitor your money?

- ❑ I don't, but I feel in control
- ❑ I don't, and it feels in disarray
- ❑ I review my bank balances & accounts regularly
- ❑ I hired a financial planner
- ❑ An Excel spreadsheet
- ❑ Other: ______________________

What is the current status of your savings?

- ❑ I have at least $1,000 worth of emergency savings in the bank.
- ❑ I have 6-8 months' worth of savings set aside for necessities (housing, food and transportation).
- ❑ I have all of the above, PLUS 6-8 months' worth of my monthly savings and investment contributions set aside.
- ❑ I am self-employed/freelancer and I have a savings account set up to make my quarterly estimated tax payments to the IRS.

How prepared are you for retirement?

- ❑ I contribute to my 401(k)
- ❑ I contribute enough to meet my full employer match.
- ❑ I have an individual retirement account (IRA) (This can be a traditional IRA, Roth, or if you're a business owner or freelancer, a SEP or SIMPLE IRA.)

Which of the following wealth-building tools do you have?

- ❑ An Incorporated company (LLC. S-corp. C-corp. Partnership)
- ❑ Term life insurance
- ❑ Whole life insurance
- ❑ Disability insurance
- ❑ A 700+ credit score
- ❑ 401K
- ❑ IRA
- ❑ Pension
- ❑ Emergency fund Financial Freedom Fund
- ❑ Investment account
- ❑ Rental real estate
- ❑ Financial planner
- ❑ Credit cards with no-to-low balance today
- ❑ An unsecured business line of credit
- ❑ Home equity
- ❑ A home equity line or credit
- ❑ A personal/business website
- ❑ A will
- ❑ An estate plan
- ❑ Access to capital (e.g. investors. parents. friends. etc)

Thank you for taking the time to answer these questions honestly. On the following pages we will go through the process of setting up your finances in a way that will keep you on track to achieve all of your financial goals. If you have any questions please feel free to email us at info@MindRightMoney.com

"Decide what kind of life you actually want then say no to everything that isn't that."

- Unknown

Deciding What You Want

Imagine going to a restaurant and telling the waiter or waitress that you're hungry but you'll take whatever is available... The waiter/waitress will say "well sir/ma'am everything on the menu is available!" Then if you proceed to ask them to choose for you then that would be very difficult because not everybody eats the same things. The point is that when you go to a restaurant you must tell the waiter based on what's available, what it is you actually want. The only way the waiter can provide you a meal is by you making a **DECISION**.

Whether you believe in the Universe, God, Buddha, The Law of Attraction, or any other higher power, you must understand that from a spiritual level, before you can command anything you must first **DECIDE** what it is you want. But even if we look at it from a practical perspective you still can't get anything in life if you don't first **DECIDE**.

I will reiterate what I said earlier... Obtaining success in anything is an exact science. There are four steps and they include:

1. Deciding what you want
2. Believing that it's possible and that you deserve it.
3. Focusing on it and visualizing it as if it's already yours
4. Paying the price by being disciplined, putting in the effort and persevering, despite any external circumstances.

And when I say success in **ANYTHING**... This includes your money too. How can you believe something is possible and that you deserve it, if you haven't **DEFINED** it? How can you focus on something and visualize that it's yours, if you haven't said what "it" is? And what are you paying the price for and being disciplined to, if again you haven't clearly **DEFINED** what it is you are being disciplined for?

Deciding what you want has to be the prerequisite in obtaining the life that you want but also in creating true financial freedom.

In the preceding section where you are asked to define your current money story, the first question that is asked is... ***"What are the 10 most important things that you want to accomplish while you're on this earth?"*** Most people that I've worked with in the past always start their answer to that question with material things like, paying off debt, buying a house, or even finding love, getting married, and having kids. While most (if not all) of these things are the greater experiences in life, the question is meant to make you go deeper than just where you are right now.

When you think about the most important things that you want to accomplish while you're on this earth, I do not want you to look at it from the lens of where you are right now. What I want you to do is to imagine that you are getting a lifetime achievement award. During the intro of your award the person doing the introduction will read your bio but it will have things that you were able to accomplish on a grand scale.

It won't talk about the kind of house you had or the car that you drove or how many vacations you went on, but instead it will give you the tangible things that impacted the world and other people.

It is my belief that if you focus on the bigger picture then the things you do day in and day out will ultimately lead you to the house, the car, the relationship, and/or the kids, but it starts with your purpose.

What will you accomplish when it's all said and done? Before we start to get into your financial goals, in this first activity, I want you to focus on writing your own lifetime achievement award.

For Example, If I were given a lifetime achievement award I would like it to read:

Ash Cash Exantus is a pioneer on the forefront of spirituality and financial education. He is a bestselling author who wrote 40+ books that have sold over 200 million copies. He sold these copies by providing the best possible book that helps and empowers anyone who reads them. He is the creator of a series of original programing that has been seen all over the world. His series helps shed light on social and financial issues. As a highly sought after paid speaker, people come to hear him speak over and over, each time touching their hearts and moving them into action. He has a nationally syndicated Talk Show and Radio show that attracts millions of daily viewers and listeners and is instrumental in creating a dialogue for Self-Improvement. All of his business ventures provide jobs and entrepreneurial opportunities for millions of people around the world. He is the recipient of a Grammy for best Audiobook, Emmy, Nobel Peace Prize and now this Lifetime Achievement Award... Ladies and gentlemen put your hands together for... Ash Cash!!!! (Crowd claps)

ACTIVITY #1 – CREATE YOUR LIFETIME ACHIEVEMENT AWARD INTRO

On the following page create your Lifetime achievement award introduction as if you won the prestigious prize and someone was going to introduce you before you went on stage. You must first create a vision statement and mission statement and your ultimate vision should be aligned with these two.

Vision = End Game

Mission = How You Will Get There

Your **Personal Vision Statement** guides your life and provides the direction necessary to live a fulfilled life.

Think of your personal vision statement as the roadmap to total bliss during your lifetime.

Your **vision statement** can be a sentence or two. For **example**, Oprah Winfrey's **vision** is: "To be a teacher. And to be known for inspiring my students to be more than they thought they could be."

Your **Personal Mission Statement** defines how you will get to your vision. Think of the vision as the GPS system but the mission is the car (AKA the vehicle that will get you to your destination)

For example, Oprah's original mission statement was...

"To uplift, enlighten, encourage and entertain through the medium of television.

My Personal Vision for my life is (Vision Statement):

I will achieve this vision by (Mission Statement):

Use the Space below to write your lifetime achievement introduction:

"If we command our wealth, we shall be rich and free. If our wealth commands us, we are poor indeed."

- Edmund Burke

Understanding Your Numbers

I am a big fan of the saying, men lie women lie numbers don't. If you want to chart a plan for the future, you have to know where you want to go. Simply knowing you want better or saying you want better won't suffice; you have to be specific about what it is you want and where you ultimately want to go.

Regardless of where you are right now It's time to open up your mind and your consciousness to assess what your ideal life looks like so you can begin to plan for it accordingly. Doing this will assure that you meet your minimum obligations while working towards what you ultimately want.

For example, if someone has a current lifestyle of $4,000 a month, but wants to live a better life, how can they plan to reach it If they do not know what that better life costs?

Given the same example, if someone's current lifestyle cost $4,000 a month and their ideal lifestyle cost $8,000 a month, this person will be better prepared to achieve their ideal because as they are living based on their current budget they can start doing the things they can do right now to start working towards that ideal budget.

Please see tasks below to begin the process:

ACTIVITY #2 - KNOW YOUR NUMBERS

What does your ideal lifestyle look like?

Would you be working if you didn't need the income? If so, what kind of work would you be doing? How many hours per week?

Who are you spending time with? How frequently are you seeing them?

What are you doing with your free time?

What city and country do you live in? Is it the same place all year round?

How many weeks per year do you travel?

How much does it cost to live your ideal lifestyle? (Please be as exact as possible. This means to look up the home prices where you want to live, the monthly expenses you will occur, etc;)

AFFIRMATIONS FOR YOUR IDEAL LIFE

I am increasingly confident in my ability to create the life I deserve

I am creating my life according to my dominant beliefs and I am improving the quality of those beliefs

I am willing to believe that I am the creator of my life experience

I am willing to believe that by focusing on feeling good I make better choices that lead to desired results

I am worthy of love, abundance, success, happiness, and fulfillment

I can do anything I put my mind to

I am successful in whatever I do

I am making things happen

I persist with confidence

I see endless opportunities before me

I'm living my full potential

I am powerfully positive in everything that I think doing say

"I remember saying to my mentor, 'If I had more money, I would have a better plan.' He quickly responded, 'I would suggest that if you had a better plan, you would have more money.' You see, it's not the amount that counts; it's the plan that counts.

-Jim Rohn

Getting S.M.A.R.T. With Your Financial Goals

Now that you know what your ideal lifestyle looks like, you need to break down your goals into short-term, midterm, and long-term perspectives. Knowing what your financial goals are and how long they will take for you to meet them will give you a blueprint on how to allocate funds for each goal.

BREAK GOALS DOWN

SHORT TERM	1-3 years
MID TERM	3-7 years
LONG TERM	7+ years

Make sure as you are creating your financial goals; you are not just listing them but making sure they are smart goals! Not smart as in intelligent but the acronym S.M.A.R.T... Meaning...

Specific

Measurable

Achievable

Realistic and

Timely.

CREATE S.M.A.R.T GOALS

SPECIFIC
MEASURABLE
ACHIEVABLE
REALISTIC
TIMELY

It's not enough to say "I want to save more money," but how much do you want to save and why do you want to save it? Is it achievable and realistic for you to save that amount based on your current circumstance? So instead of "I want to save more money," a S.M.A.R.T. goal will say, "I am going to save $5,000 into my Financial Freedom Fund (FFF) by this time next year.

ACTIVITY #3 - BREAKDOWN YOUR FINANCIAL GOALS

CREATE A 10-YEAR VISION, A 5-YEAR VISION, AND 1-YEAR GOALS

Now that you have your ideal life thought through, what does that look like in 10 years?

What does your life need to look like in 5 years so that you can be where you want to be in 10 years?

What do you need to accomplish this year to get to your 5-year vision?

Short-Term Goals

1.

2.

3.

4.

5.

6.

7.

Mid-Term Goals

1.

2.

3.

4.

5.

6.

7.

Long-Term Goals

1.

2.

3.

4.

5.

6.

7.

"The habit of saving is itself an education; it fosters every virtue, teaches self-denial, cultivates the sense of order, trains to forethought, and so broadens the mind"

– Thomas T. Munger

Creating Your Financial Freedom Fund (The Right Way)

Many people save for emergencies but because we know that words have power we will no longer call our savings an "Emergency fund." Our goal going forward is to build financial freedom so our savings should be called a Financial Freedom Fund (FFF). Setting up your FFF starts with knowing your numbers. How much money does it take for you to meet all of your basic needs? Take that number and multiply it by six then by eight. Those two numbers are the minimum and maximum financial goals for your financial freedom fund.

ACTIVITY #4 – CREATE A FINANCIAL FREEDOM FUND

How to
Build an ~~Emergency Fund~~
Financial Freedom Fund

1 Put aside a set amount
2 Make it automatic
3 Make it inconvenient
4 Forget about it

The following are four steps on how to build a financial freedom fund.

1. Put aside a set amount

As I stated earlier, the goal should be to save 6 to 8 months of expenses in an account. To get to this amount you should set aside a set amount each month to go to your bank account directly. The amount you save could be a dollar amount, or it can be a percentage; the preference is really up to you. I prefer doing a percentage; that way, the amount you save increases as your income increases.

2. Make it automatic

Most people fail at saving money because they rely on themselves to activate the savings. What I found is that when you make savings automatic, it will happen because you have removed yourself out of the equation.

Set it and forget it! This must be done before you receive your check or deposit; meaning that you are paying yourself first. Similar to how IRS income tax comes out of your paycheck, (if you work a 9 to 5) before you even receive a dollar... This is how I want you to treat yourself now. The IRS is not more important than you!

3. Make it inconvenient

Another reason why people fail to save or are unsuccessful at saving is because they have their savings account in the same bank that has their checking account. This means that every time they look at their checking account balance, they'll also be reminded that they have some money saved in savings.

Most will show restraint at the beginning of their saving journey but eventually once the "Buy One, Get One Free" sales become frequent, that will power fades and saving starts to deplete. This is why I want you to make it inconvenient for you to access your Financial Freedom Fund (FFF). This means that your savings account should not be at the same bank that you have your primary checking account. It should be at a high yielding online bank, regional bank, or credit union. With the lack of access available to you by using one of these financial institutions, the chances of your savings building to 6 to 8 months of expenses are greater.

4. Forget about it

Lastly, you should forget that this account even exists. The more you have it in your consciousness that you have money set aside for a rainy day, the more you will attract situations that will force you to use it.

As you forget about this account even existing, you are giving it a better chance of growing to its full potential. Eventually, as this account grows, you can continue the same savings habit, but instead of directing the funds towards savings you can use it to invest.

NOTES

"Money is only a tool. It will take you wherever you wish, but it will not replace you as the driver."

– Ayn Rand

Telling Your Money What To Do & How To Do It

Telling your money what to do comes down to budgeting your money properly. Before you create your budget, you must first imagine it then implement. When I say "Imagine then implement" what I'm saying is to make sure that as you are putting your budget together, it is something that you can see yourself implementing. I can't begin to tell you the number of people I know that put budgets together who knew from day one they were not going to follow.

ACTIVITY #5 – VISUALIZE, CREATE, AND IMPLEMENT YOUR BUDGET

So here are steps to creating a budget:

1. Get all of your relevant documents together. This should include all financial statements, investments, pay stubs, dividends, annuities, child support, alimony, everything! Anything you pay out each month and everything you receive as income! This will help you get organized to create the budget accurately and truly understand your bottom line.

   Bottom Line = Income - Expenses

2. Determine how you will record your budget. You can either use a blank piece of paper, the below template, or an excel spreadsheet. Once you decide, write down all the sources of income that you receive.

3. Write down all of your expenses in the expense column recording everything that has to be paid each month. First and foremost recording your "pay yourself first" money. Then your mortgage or rent, car payment or transportation, insurance payments, food, utilities, entertainment, dry cleaning, laundry, etc.;

4. Break down your expenses into two categories: fixed and variable. Fixed expenses are expenses that don't change from month to month. Variable expenses are expenses that can vary depending on usage (make sure that you monitor your variable expenses so that they don't go over a certain amount each month).

5. Total up all of your income and expenses, making sure that expenses aren't greater than income. If income is higher than expenses; congratulations, you have a positive bottom line and more money to save and invest. If expenses are greater than income, than your bottom line is negative, and you must adjust.

   There are only three ways that you can increase your bottom line.

   1) Cut Expenses

   2) Increase Income or

   3) Do both!

   To cut expenses; first, try to minimize or limit things that are not a necessity (never adjust your "Financial Freedom Fund")

6. You must review your budget monthly and make all the necessary adjustments as your life changes. It is irresponsible to think that your expenses are just going to remain the same from month to month. Keep a watchful eye and again stay honest!

Creating and following a budget can make the difference between worrying about money and living stress-free! Your budget is your first practical tool that will determine how serious you are about living financially free! You can't get to a destination if you don't know where you're going!

As you are preparing your budget, if you find that you are going over and need to cut some expenses out, here are some questions you should ask yourself:

Do I really need it?

If I get it, how long will I use it?

How long will I enjoy it?

Are there other ways to get it? Borrow, buy it used, cheaper, split with a friend.

What if I don't get it? With my life still, be OK?

Personal Monthly Budget

MINDRIGHT
MONEY MANAGEMENT

INCOME	Budget	Actual	Difference
Wages & Tips			-
Interest Income			-
Dividends			-
Gifts Received			-
Refunds/Reimbursements			-
Transfer From Savings			-
Other			-
Other			-
Total INCOME	-	-	-

HOME EXPENSES	Budget	Actual	Difference
Mortgage/Rent			-
Home/Rental Insurance			-
Electricity			-
Gas/Oil			-
Water/Sewer/Trash			-
Phone			-
Cable/Satellite			-
Internet			-
Furnishings/Appliances			-
Lawn/Garden			-
Maintenance/Supplies			-
Improvements			-
Other			-
Total HOME EXPENSES	-	-	-

TRANSPORTATION	Budget	Actual	Difference
Vehicle Payments			-
Auto Insurance			-
Fuel			-
Bus/Taxi/Train Fare			-
Repairs			-
Registration/License			-
Other			-
Total TRANSPORTATION	-	-	-

HEALTH	Budget	Actual	Difference
Health Insurance			-
Doctor/Dentist			-
Medicine/Drugs			-
Health Club Dues			-
Life Insurance			-
Veterinarian/Pet Care			-
Other			-
Total HEALTH	-	-	-

CHARITY/GIFTS	Budget	Actual	Difference
Gifts Given			-
Charitable Donations			-
Religious Donations			-
Other			-
Total CHARITY/GIFTS	-	-	-

SUBSCRIPTIONS	Budget	Actual	Difference
Newspaper			-
Magazines			-
Dues/Memberships			-
Other			-
Total SUBSCRIPTIONS	-	-	-

MONTHLY BUDGET SUMMARY	Budget	Actual	Difference
Total Income			-
Total Expenses			-
NET			

DAILY LIVING	Budget	Actual	Difference
Groceries			-
Personal Supplies			-
Clothing			-
Cleaning			-
Education/Lessons			-
Dining/Eating Out			-
Salon/Barber			-
Pet Food			-
Other			-
Total DAILY LIVING	-	-	-

ENTERTAINMENT	Budget	Actual	Difference
Netflix			-
myfico			-
Games			-
Rentals			-
Movies/Theater			-
Concerts/Plays			-
Books			-
Hobbies			-
Film/Photos			-
Sports			-
Outdoor Recreation			-
Toys/Gadgets			-
Vacation/Travel			-
Other			-
Total ENTERTAINMENT	-	-	-

SAVINGS	Budget	Actual	Difference
Emergency Fund			-
Transfer to Savings			-
Retirement (401k, IRA)			-
Investments			-
Education			-
Spending $$			-
Total SAVINGS	-	-	-

OBLIGATIONS	Budget	Actual	Difference
Student Loan			-
Other Loan			-
Credit Cards			-
Alimony/Child Support			-
Federal Taxes			-
State/Local Taxes			-
Other			-
Total OBLIGATIONS	-	-	-

MISCELLANEOUS	Budget	Actual	Difference
Bank Fees			-
Postage			-
Other			-
Other			-
Total MISCELLANEOUS	-	-	-

"If you don't find a way to make money while you sleep, you will work until you die"

- Warren Buffett

Diversifying Your Income

Studies show that the average millionaire has seven streams of income. If you are looking for true financial freedom, then you must not live off of just one stream of income. Doing so is committing economic suicide. Because you may not have come from a trust fund, you may have to start working to accumulate funds before financial freedom can be built but that's why I say to begin active, but eventually, you need that relationship to switch and allow passive income to be your best friend.

What's the difference between active income and passive income?

Active income is when you trade time for money. For example, if you work a 9 to 5 job, you are investing a considerable amount of time in exchange for a paycheck every week, bi-weekly, bi-monthly, or monthly. If you stop working, you don't get paid. So, in essence, your time equals money.

Passive income, on the other hand, is getting money without having to trade your time. You may have to put in a lot of time during the initial setup, but after that time is invested, money keeps flowing even while you sleep. For example, you invest in stock and that stock pays you a dividend quarterly without you doing much, you rent out an apartment you own and receive monthly income without lifting a finger, or you write a book, and that book pays you royalties each month.

In this case, you invest your time only during the initial set up. The product or service you developed during that time starts earning money for you over a period of time (mostly in perpetuity) without you investing much time further.

ACTIVITY #6 – DIVERSIFYING YOUR INCOME

The following is how to diversify your income and create multiple streams:

Start with Active... Build up Passive!!!

1 Work to learn + Earn

2 Use knowledge to solve a problem

3 Use Money to Make Money

4 Repeat!

1. Work to learn + Earn

Most people get a job to earn money, but that is the worst use of time if that's all you're getting. To diversify your income, you have to make sure that while you are working, you are also learning a skill that is transferable as an entrepreneur. Make sure that what you are doing to earn money teaches you lessons that you can monetize off now and/or later.

2. Use knowledge to solve a problem

With your newfound knowledge, it is time to use it to solve a problem. In fact, a problem solver is the definition of an entrepreneur: someone who gets paid to solve a problem. Whether you do this full-time or on the side, understand that your knowledge is valuable and that's what's going to begin the process of earning you an income independent of your 9-5 or contract work.

3. Use Money to Make Money

Now that you have started to accumulate money, instead of using that money to buy things, use that money to purchase income-producing assets. These income-producing assets are going to be your multiple streams of income.

4. Repeat!

Now it's time to repeat the process.

1. Work to learn and earn
2. Use your knowledge to solve a problem
3. Use the money you make from solving your problem to make more money by investing in another income-producing asset.

Repeating this process will give you everything you need to create financial freedom.

Below are the Common Types of (Passive) Streams of Income

1. Interest – from a variety of loans, either to individuals (peer to peer lending or private notes) or companies (bonds, notes)
2. Dividends – from investments, partnerships
3. Capital gains – from the sale of investments
4. Royalties – from products you sell or license
5. Rental income – from real estate
6. Business income – which may or may not be passive but the idea is you build something that generates income without active work, like a website or the sale of information products

Below you will find a list of passive income ideas. If you need help developing your idea please apply for our program at www.MailBoxMoneyAcademy.com

Top 50 Passive Income Ideas

- Write a Book
- Publish an E-book
- Start a Blog
- Store People's Stuff
- Create an Online Course
- Build an Affiliate Marketing Niche Site
- Robo-Investing
- Real Estate Investment Trusts (REITs)
- High-Yield Dividend Stocks & Funds
- Peer to Peer (P2P) Lending
- Private Equity Funds
- Sublease Apartment or House
- Rent Your Car or Parking Space
- Transcription
- Buy Royalties
- Start a Podcast
- Refinance Your Mortgage
- Start an E-commerce Business
- Buy an Existing Business
- Outsourcing Your Business
- Laundromat
- Vending Machines
- Start a YouTube Channel
- Stock Photos
- Buy and Sell Domain Names for Websites
- Create Software or an App
- Manage Social Media Accounts
- Become a Host on Airbnb
- Financial Reward Programs
- Become an Angel Investor
- Inventory Investment for Small Businesses
- Invest in a Food Truck
- Rent Personal Items
- Rent Out Old Baby Gear
- Lease Equipment
- Sell Retargeting Advertisements
- Freelance Graphic Design

- Sell Your Clothes
- Start an Etsy Store
- Become a Notary
- Customer Interviews
- Raw Land Flipping
- Become a Brand Ambassador
- House Sitting
- Vehicle Advertising
- Consulting
- Design Logos
- Be an Extra in Movies
- Email Marketing
- Create an Audiobook

"A person who dies without adequate protection for their family should have to come back and see the mess they created"

- *Will Rogers*

Protecting Everything You Love

Imagine building a successful retail store from scratch then not locking your doors at night and allowing looters to come in and steal all of your inventory. Imagine building a home from the ground up and not covering it up and allowing mother nature to destroy what you just built. This is exactly what we do when we don't take the time to protect our assets adequately. Using insurance, we can begin to protect our assets; here's how:

Insurance, in its simplest terms, means "Just in Case." It provides you peace of mind in the form of monetary compensation just in case something happens. Life insurance specifically is an agreement between you and an insurance company which states that in return for your monthly payments they agree to provide any person or persons you choose, called beneficiaries, a lump sum of money in the case of your demise.

After someone dies, many things need to be taken care of, such as funeral arrangements, taxes, mortgage payments, car loans, credit card debts, and other expenses. The most common use of life insurance is to supplement the loss of income that occurs. When you die, and your money stops coming in, besides the grief that comes with the loss, your family may be left with limited resources, which cause additional stress and anguish. Life insurance alleviates that and allows life to go on after the death of a loved one.

While most people use life insurance to cover final expenses, it can also be used to cover sending children to college and maintaining your family's lifestyle. The amount of insurance needed depends on a few variables which include your marital status, the size of your family, what expenses you have, what stage of your career you are in and what your goals and aspirations are. There are many types of life insurances, and the costs are determined by many factors, which include age, sex, and health.

Simply put, you can purchase life insurance with a death benefit large enough to cover all of the expenses that may come up after death; like estate taxes, mortgages, creditors, etc.:

Some other forms of asset protection include:

HOMEOWNERS INSURANCE.

For most people owning a home is going to be the single most significant investment that they make. Homeowners insurance is what protects this significant investment against fire and flood, but that's not all it does. Homeowners insurance can also protect you against any potential lawsuits.

If someone were to get injured on your property and decided that they were going to sue you, without homeowners insurance they can attack all of your assets. With homeowners insurance, any liability coverage that you have would protect you and your assets.

AUTO INSURANCE.

The same thing applies for auto insurance. If you are involved in a car accident that results in a lawsuit without the proper coverage your assets can be in jeopardy. Many people in an attempt to save money will settle for the minimum legal liability coverage on their auto insurance policy, but trying to save a few dollars now can potentially cost you later.

A great way to accomplish this protection is to look into getting umbrella liability insurance. This will cover you if someone is trying to attack your assets.

For example, if someone was involved in a car accident and their liability coverage wasn't enough to cover all of the expenses, the umbrella policy can pick up and pay what's needed.

So for this example, if someone had a $1 million auto liability policy and were sued for $2 million the umbrella policy would pay the additional $1 million instead of having their assets or wages garnished.

LONG-TERM CARE INSURANCE.

Lastly, long-term care insurance is an integral part of asset protection. In the event of sickness, healthcare policies won't cover everything... Especially if it is a long-term illness or disability.

Long-term care insurance pays for medical expenses that you would typically have to pay out of pocket when your health insurance stopped covering it. Without long-term care insurance, these expenses would have to be paid by liquidating your assets.

Asset protection is a critical part of your financial plan. Make sure you are protected accurately by reaching out to a qualified insurance agent, company representative, or financial advisor.

ACTIVITY #7 - ACQUIRE ASSET PROTECTION

Visit www.MindRightInsurance.com to set up an appointment with one of our Insurance Agents so they can give you a quote for proper coverage on you and your loved ones.

If you are interested in other ways to use insurance to build wealth for you and your family please visit www.FamilyWealthSecrets.com

"Think What You Do When You Run in Debt: You Give to Another Power over Your Liberty."

- Benjamin Franklin

MINDRIGHT
MONEY MANAGEMENT

Creating A Debt Elimination Plan

I don't know two ways to say this, but having debt is dumb and counter-intuitive to financial freedom and building wealth! Even though I understand why many of us decide to get into debt, it is still foolish. The only caveat to this statement is if the debt is being used to purchase assets or increase your net-worth.

In my book The Wake-Up Call: Financial Inspiration Learned from 444 + A Step by Step Guide on How to Implement Each Financial Principle; I give a real-life example of the good use of debt using Jay-Z and Beyoncé.

Case in point: Jay-Z and Beyoncé used credit themselves to leverage their wealth in a real way. Even though they are worth more than a billion dollars combined, they took out a $52.8 million mortgage for their Bel-Air mansion. Using a blind trust, they paid $88million for their beautiful estate and financed the rest of the $135 million home.

You may be asking why wouldn't they just pay cash for the whole home? Well with historically low mortgage rates, taking out a loan allows them to put their money to better use. To drive the point home; let's say they are paying 4% on their $52.8 million mortgage, if they are able to invest that $52.8 million of their own cash in something that is paying 10% they are better off because the $528,000 they would make on the interest would easily pay the $211,000 interest payment from the mortgage; leaving them with a profit of $317,000 x 30 years = $9,510,000 which is the amount of money they made by using someone else's money... GENIUS!!!!

Many finance experts will tell you that a business loan, mortgage, and student loan are "Good Debt" but unless you have a tangible way (like the example above) to make it build wealth, then I don't agree. I suggest that if you have outstanding debt use the method below to get rid of it, then commit to a debt-free life:

SNOWBALL YOUR DEBT

Most people concentrating on paying down debt think about the most logical step, which is to pay down the debt that has the highest interest rate. But snowballing debt is actually the opposite.

Many financial advisors cringe at this, but I (including some other reputable folks) say FORGET the interest rate! Managing debt and your finances is just as psychological as it is practical. The concept of snowballing debt is simply paying down your smallest debt first, then using the money from the paid off debt to tackle the next lowest.

Doing this gives you some small victories early on, which helps build the perception that you are making progress. No matter what the interest rates are, if you have ten credit accounts and you can pay off three of them in a matter of months, it gives you the confidence and motivation you need to succeed.

ACTIVITY #8 – CREATING YOUR BAD-DEBT ELIMINATION PLAN

Steps to snowballing debt:

1. Using the sheet on the next page list all of your debts in order, from the smallest to the largest. Again, FORGET about the interest rate! (The only time you should be concerned with the rate is if two debts have the same or similar payoff balances. In that instance pay off the debt with the highest rate).

2. Pay the minimum payment on all of your debts except for the smallest one. With what you have leftover, pay down the lowest as much as you can and as fast as you can. Every time you get any extra money, you need to keep paying the smallest debt until it disappears.

3. Every time a debt is paid off, add whatever you were paying as its minimum payment to your next debt payment, plus any extra amount available.

4. Redo the sheet every time you pay off a debt so that you can see how close you are to being debt-free! Make sure you keep the old sheets as a reminder too!

Debt Snowball

Attacking Your Debt, One Account at a Time

Step 1

List your debts in order from the smallest Total Payoff balance to the largest. Don't be concerned with interest rates, unless two debts have a similar payoff balance. In that case, list the one with the higher interest rate first.

DEBTS	TOTAL PAYOFF
Diagnostic	50
Hospital Bill	460
Home Depot	770

Step 2

Attack that smallest debt by paying as much on it as you possibly can. Once you pay one debt off, take what you were paying on that one and add it to the minimum payment of the next debt. As the snowball rolls over, it picks up more snow. Get it?

MIN. PAYMENT		NEW PAYMENT
~~19~~		~~19~~
~~38~~	+	~~48~~
45	=	93

Step 3

Every time you pay off a debt, cross the debt off. This will show you how close you're getting to becoming debt free.

~~Hospital Bill~~
~~Home Depot~~
~~Chase VISA~~
~~Car Loan~~
I'M DEBT-FREE!!!!!

List your debts smallest to largest by balance

Once a debt is paid off, add the next minimum payment to your current amount. This becomes the new payment.

DEBTS	TOTAL PAYOFF	MIN. PAYMENT	NEW PAYMENT

MINDRIGHT
MONEY MANAGEMENT

"Unity is strength... when there is teamwork and collaboration, wonderful things can be achieved.

- Mattie Stepanek

Creating Your Money Accountability Team

This step is both spiritual and practical. Napoleon Hill introduced the concept of the mastermind alliance in the classic book, Think and Grow Rich, and is the process of combining like minds to create a greater force.

Hill defines it as "The coordination of knowledge and effort of two or more people, who work toward a definite purpose, in the spirit of harmony." Forming a Mastermind group and assembling your money team is imperative in your quest for financial freedom.

So, who should be part of your money team?

The professional you need on your money team will vary depending on your current income level, which I will breakdown into three categories:

MindRight™ Wealth Starter = People who make $30,000 per year or less

MindRight™ Wealth Chaser = People who make between $30,000 - $150,000

MindRight™ Wealth Builder = People who make above $150,000

If I start with the MindRight™ Wealth Builder, who makes $150,000 or more, their money team consists of private bankers, wealth advisors/financial advisors, accountants, and business managers. They will also have an attorney who helps them with all legal matters including trust, estate planning, etc.;

The private banker will be the one who manages their deposit accounts. Sometimes a private banker may give suggestions on investments but not often. That is the job of the wealth advisor/financial advisor to give their clients access to investments that will help grow their wealth over time. They also have access to accountants that help them determine what are the tax implications of their financial decisions as well as filing their taxes.

Lastly, many who fall under the MindRight™ Wealth Builders category have business managers and investment bankers who help them manage the day-to-day operations of their business but also bring them business opportunities that they can also invest in.

For the MindRight™ Wealth Chaser, who makes between $30,000 and 150,000 they will need a banker, A financial advisor, and an accountant.

For the MindRight™ Wealth Starter who makes less than $30,000 a year they will most likely only have a banker and a tax preparer but should have a financial coach or financial counselor who can help them manage their money better.

Regardless of income level, all individuals who are serious about creating and maintaining financial freedom should be part of a money mastermind group.

Each person in the group serves as an accountability partner for one another. They challenge each other to set powerful goals and push each other to accomplish them.

Masterminding is about commitment, confidentiality, willingness to give and receive advice and ideas, and the support of one another with total honesty, respect, and compassion. Spending time with this person/group will undoubtedly move you closer to ALL of your dreams and aspirations.

ACTIVITY #9 - CREATING YOUR MONEY ACCOUNTABILITY TEAM

Below, makes a list of the characteristics you would like in an accountability partner. Begin to identify those who fit the description. If you do not currently know someone that fits, begin putting yourself out there to meet this person. Start a weekly mastermind call or meeting in person if possible. Also, join our private group at www.MindRightMastermind.com.

Money Accountability Partner #1:

Money Accountability Partner #2:

Money Accountability Partner #3:

Financial Coach/Financial Counselor:

Tax Preparer:

Personal Banker/Private Banker:

Business Banker:

Financial Advisor:

Business Manager:

Investment Banker:

Tax Preparer:

Accountant:

Attorney:

“How many millionaires do you know who have become wealthy by investing in savings accounts? I rest my case.“

- Robert G. Allen

Investing In Your Now To Build Your Future

As we stated previously, (and will continue to reiterate) one of our main goals as it relates to financial freedom is to change our relationship with money. We want to go from working hard for it to it working hard for us. Investing in stocks, bonds, mutual funds, etc.; are smart and efficient ways to build wealth and live the life of our dreams.

It's imperative to realize that investing is about long-term growth. Many people have this misconception (especially in poor households) that investing is like gambling; this could not be further from the truth. Gambling is about hoping you will win a bet that has a big pay-off in a short amount of time while investing is about committing your money for the long-term in exchange for a calculated financial return.

Gambling is arbitrary with no real strategy needed; it's merely the luck of the draw. Investing, on the other hand, happens through years of research and risk evaluation, which gives the investor a better probability of positive returns over the long haul.

To be successful at investing it requires you to know how much risk you can or should take on (Risk Tolerance), Knowledge of the options available to you, a clear vision of your financial goals, and a realistic view of where you are right now. You also have to regularly monitor your collection of investments, which are better known as your portfolio to make sure you are still in line with your financial objectives.

There are three main reasons why investing is essential: 1) Compound Interest, 2) The Power of Time, and 3) to offset inflation:

1) COMPOUND INTEREST

The power of compound interest can grow your money exponentially and allow you to add another stream of passive income to your financial arsenal.

Compound interest is earning interest on your principal plus previously accumulated interest. For example: I lend you $100 at 10% interest, and you pay me back $110. The following month I lend you the $110, and you pay me back $121. I just earned interest off of the $10 I made off you the first month, allowing my money to grow faster. This is making your money work for you at its finest. The more, the merrier so, the more you invest, the better this concept works.

2) THE POWER OF TIME

The sooner you start investing your money, the more it will grow because of the ability to take advantage of compound interest. Many people find excuses why not to invest but again investing is about the long term, so the longer you delay, the more you lose. If you were to invest $500 a month for 20 years, with an interest rate of 11%, your money would grow to about $400,000. If you invested that same $500 a month for 30 years with the same rate, your money would grow to about $1,402,250! See illustration below:

As you can see, because of compound interest and the power of time you can quadruple your money in ten years and increase it by more than fourteenfold in twenty. Procrastination has a high cost, and unfortunately, it comes in the form of hard cold cash! Stop waiting! You have nothing to lose, so put that money to work!

3) OFFSET INFLATION

If you looked in the dictionary for the meaning of inflation, it would say that it's "The rate of increase of a price index as a percentage rate of change in price level over time." Huh?? Unless you have a degree in economics then nine times out of ten that definition sounds like a foreign language, so in simpler terms, inflation is the rate of decrease in your purchasing power.

To break it down even further, inflation is the reason why you pay $1 for a cup of coffee that used to cost $.50 or why years ago $5 could buy you a whole meal, but now it can only buy you one drink (if that). What we were able to purchase yesterday with a dollar now cost us more today!

The average rate of inflation is now about 3%, which means that on average, your dollar is worth $.03 less every year. It also means that investing your money wisely is essential to protect your purchasing power.

At a minimum, your goal should be at least to keep pace with inflation, so your money doesn't lose its value. Don't think that's important? Then consider this, if inflation is 3% and you have $10,000 sitting in an account earning only 1% then technically you're losing 2% per year.

To break it down even further that means in ten years your $10,000 will be worth only $8,000. To take it another step you are losing even more because of the compound interest you could've earned on the 2% you're losing (but I will spare you with the calculations).

The moral of the story is this; start investing as soon as possible; you have more to gain to do it and even more to lose if you don't!

THINGS TO CONSIDER WHEN INVESTING

Often, when I conduct workshops and seminars one of the first questions that I always get, is "How do I double my money?" or "I have money saved up, what should I invest in?" Before you even consider investing a dollar, you must first understand your money habits, personality, pressures that you succumb to and your current financial picture. After that's established, you need to figure out where you are trying to go and begin setting goals as well as a budget for investing.

ASSESSING YOUR RISK TOLERANCE

Some people believe that to make it big; you have to risk big or spend big. You know the saying, "Scared money don't make money." These folks are comfortable taking risk.

Others can't sleep a wink if they think for one second their money is at risk of being lost. Knowing your risk tolerance is essential in helping you invest in products that not only make economic sense but emotional sense as well. I am a big believer in the law of attraction and as the law says, "What you resist will persist." Not being comfortable with your investment choices and worrying about losing money will only make that inevitable.

Answer the following questions, either "True" or "False" to learn more about your comfort level:

1. I prefer to have my savings in cash or in the bank's FDIC insured products than to risk losing it in the stock market
2. People who invest in the stock market are reckless.
3. I don't like it when I have to make major financial decisions.
4. Better safe than sorry is a saying that I live by, so having my money safe is more important to me than the possibility of big returns.
5. I watch my money carefully, and if I were to invest, I would adjust my portfolio often if there were ever any signs that my account was decreasing in value.
6. A "great investment opportunity" means nothing to me.
7. Losing any money whatsoever makes me very mad.
8. I need to have access to my money at all times.
9. I hate gambling.
10. I make sure that I do my research before I put my money into anything. I never make decisions based on a gut feeling.

The more you answered "True," the more conservative you are as an investor, meaning that you don't like taking too many risks. Being conservative is neither good nor bad; just don't allow it to stop you from investing. No matter what your risk tolerance is, you must begin to invest your money to grow it and become financially free.

Generally, the lower the risk, the lower the reward, and vice versa (the higher the risk, the higher the reward. Make sure when choosing an investment strategy, it is based on your expected returns.

The younger you are the more risk-tolerant you should be because of your longer earning ability, but my suggestion for anyone who is just starting is to ease in and get comfortable before you jump in with both feet! As I said earlier, investing isn't gambling if you do it right; it's about taking calculated risks that will increase your wealth in the long run.

RISK VS. REWARD AND HOW TO HANDLE IT

Everything that you can possibly invest in comes with some level of risk; Nothing is guaranteed. Not only is there a possibility that you might not make any profit, but there is also the possibility of losing some or even all of your investment. As a wealth coach, it would've been irresponsible of me not to give you this disclosure, but now that we've gotten that out of the way, there are proven ways in which you can manage your risk to increase the probability of a profit.

Many who are skeptical of the stock market are going to point out the few times that the stock market has crashed or how Enron and Bernie Madoff lost billions of dollars for hard-working citizens. Unfortunately, those people are right but also those people are probably not wealthy.

I don't say this to say that investing in the stock market is the only way to be financially free, but it is an essential component to building wealth. The following are a few of the aforementioned proven techniques that will help mitigate your risk when investing:

ASSET ALLOCATION

The first step in reducing your risk is to make sure you are practicing asset allocation. Just like a mutual fund asset allocation is about "not putting all your eggs in one basket." This means that while investing, you should have money in the different types of asset classes, which are cash, stocks, and bonds. Doing this is a proactive way of securing your investments.

Typically, when stocks are doing well, bonds aren't, and vice versa. Having some money in a cash equivalent is also a way to protect your capital as well. Besides the risk of inflation, there isn't any way that you can lose money in a cash equivalent.

If we had to put the asset classes in order from risky to less risky, it would be stocks, then bonds, then cash. The potential reward for each are in that order as well; the riskier the investment, the higher the potential reward.

Where you decide to allocate your money is going to depend on your risk tolerance, so make sure that whatever you choose, you are going to be comfortable with the decision. You must also make sure that your asset allocation will be in line with your financial objectives.

DIVERSIFICATION

Once you have the right mix of the different asset classes, you can mitigate your risk even further by using Diversification. Within the stock and bond families, some are riskier than others. As we know now, the higher the risk, the greater the reward and vice versa, so diversification is about investing your money in different types of risk levels within the asset classes.

Just in case I confused you, I mean that if you are investing in stock or bonds, then a portion should be in the risky type that has the potential for greater reward and another piece should be in the less risky type that has the least potential of going down. The percentage in which you decide to invest in each type all depends again on your risk tolerance and comfort level. The simple way to achieve this is with mutual funds since they come prepackaged with different asset classes and risk types.

DOLLAR-COST AVERAGING

Another technique that helps with mitigating risk is called dollar-cost averaging. Dollar-cost averaging is the process of purchasing investments with a fixed amount of money regularly. Doing this allows you to buy more shares when prices are low and less when prices are high, which ultimately reduces your overall cost of investing.

For example, if I had $10,000 to invest and did so at one time, I am entering the market at $10,000, so my investment can either go up or down. So assuming a stock price is $100 per share and goes up to $110 then I will be up by $1000 in total.

Let say the next month the stock goes down to $80 then my total investment would be worth $8000 because all my money was invested at once.

But what if I broke that $10,000 down to $1,000 a month for ten months? That means that if a stock is $100 a share at my beginning point, I would purchase ten at $100 and if it went down to $80, I would now purchase 12 shares at the new price and not lose money but instead gain in the number of shares I can buy.

If the stock goes up to $110 the following month I would purchase 9 instead of the 12 but now that means that the 10 I bought in month one for $100 a share has gained $100 ($10 increase x 10 shares) and the 12 I bought in month two for $80 a share has gained $360 ($30 increase per share x 12 shares).

This method does not make you rich faster but removes the risk of losing it all at one time. To be fair, though, it also removes the opportunity to gain it all at one time as well, but for the long haul, it is smarter investing if you are risk-averse.

WHERE TO START

So the million-dollar question is, "I have some money, how do I invest?" To start, you would need to open a brokerage account either at your financial institution or with a traditional or discount broker.

Prior to 1999, there was something called the Glass-Steagall Act, which prohibited Deposit banks from selling investment products and vice verse. This act was repealed in 1999, so today you can walk into your bank or credit union and purchase investment products. Most banks usually have a financial adviser on staff that will help you with making investment decisions at no cost.

A brokerage firm like Charles Schwab, TD Ameritrade, Fidelity, Vanguard, or E*Trade can provide a wide range of services. You also have Robo-advisers like Robinhood, Wealthfront, Betterment, Wealthsimple that can get you started economically.

How you receive that service will determine how much you pay. A traditional broker provides you with professional money managers who will help you with investment advice for a fee. Because of this personal attention given, a traditional brokerage house will tend to be more expensive.

A discount broker and Robo-advisers, on the other hand, are the best solution for those who feel they can invest without the need for professional assistance. Discount brokers do charge when you make a trade, but the cost is considerably less than having a money manager help you.

Once you open your brokerage account, you can begin to buy and sell your stocks, bonds, and cash equivalents or securities for short. No matter what option you choose, most mediums allow you to trade in person, over the phone, or online.

Robo-advisers give you the sophistication of having a money manager, but instead, decisions are made through artificial intelligence and increase your odds of success since the computer is analyzing millions of options to give you the best one.

Overall the decisions you make while investing your money should be sound and not based on emotion. Do your research, hire competent advisers, and trust your knowledge coupled with your adviser's recommendation.

There's a difference between being paranoid and being cautious. Paranoia is a negative state of being based on things that are not real or may not happen. Being careful is about knowing all the facts before fully committing into anything. Be cautious! Understand what you are getting into and ask as many questions as needed for you to be comfortable.

ACTIVITY #10 - INVEST IN YOUR NOW & BUILD YOUR FUTURE

Use these questions to help you start thinking about investments — even if you don't have any just yet.

How much do you have available to invest on a monthly basis? Be honest with your budget at this point in time. You can adjust it later, but what could you set aside right now toward investing?

$____________________

What income investments do you have currently (for example, a property that you own and rent out to others)?

Do you currently invest in your employer's retirement plan (e.g., 401(k) or 403(b) plan)?

- ❑ Yes
- ❑ No
- ❑ N/A

How much do you contribute and how often (e.g., 6 percent per paycheck)?

$___ Per ______________

Does your employer offer a matching contribution?

- ❑ Yes
- ❑ No

What is the maximum amount your employer will match?

____%

Are you currently contributing up to the maximum employer match?

- ❑ Yes
- ❑ No

Research and choose an online discount brokers then list below

____

____

____

____

____

"Your story is the greatest legacy that you will leave to your friends. It's the longest-lasting legacy you will leave to your heirs."

- *Steve Saint*

Setting Up Your Family's Legacy

We often hear the term "Generational Wealth" tossed around a lot, but what does that mean and how does one build it? It is often just understood that generational wealth is monetary but that is just a piece of it.

Your family legacy plan is going to be done in three stages. First you must understand who you are by creating a family tree and collect the stories of all of your ancestors from your eldest living relatives, then you will write your own personal story to be passed down to your descendants, and lastly you will create a traditional estate plan to pass down your assets. Why is your family tree and personal story important? Wealth is spiritual! If you don't know who you are then it is impossible to build true wealth.

WHAT IS A FAMILY TREE?

A family tree is the most common form of visually documenting one's ancestry. Most family tree charts include a box for each individual and each box is connected to the others to indicate relationships. In addition to an individual's name, each box may include dates, birthplace, and other information, depending on the desired complexity of the family tree diagram.

Typically, a generation is organized into a single level so it's easy to see at a glance which ancestors preceded which generation because they are physically above them on the tree.

A horizontal line between two boxes indicates a marriage. A bracket from a couple to a lower set of boxes indicates the children from that marriage. Although most family trees grow vertically, they are occasionally drawn sideways, as well.

WHAT IS A WILL?

A will is a document that provides specific instructions regarding the disposition of a person's property and assets after they die. One important note or exception to the rule is that there are other assets such as life insurance, retirement accounts, and jointly owned property that pass to beneficiaries without a will.

When most people hear the words "will," "trust," or "estate planning," they automatically think that these are things reserved for millionaires and billionaires. This couldn't be the furthest thing from the truth: regardless of how much money you have, you must have a plan for what will happen to your assets and who should receive the things you own after you leave this earth.

An estate plan can be something as simple as having life insurance for your family and naming a beneficiary for your retirement accounts, or as complicated as having several trusts for different purposes in addition to your will. Regardless of what direction you decide to go, you must put a transition plan in place to maintain the continuity of your family business that outlives you.

Estate planning is more than just having a will. It is a plan that is put in place to lessen the financial impact of your death on those you leave behind.

At a minimum, estate planning is for the benefit and care of your loved ones, making the legal and financial issues more comfortable to deal with if you pass away. But it is also a tool to transfer wealth and maintain your family legacy. Every competent adult should have a succession plan, aka an estate plan, especially if you have children.

Problems with probate, creditors, con artists, lawsuits, lawyers, and death taxes can all delay the settlement of your estate, but without a proper plan in place, you can jeopardize your wishes.

If you die without a will you die "intestate." When this happens, relatives of the deceased have to go through probate court to claim ownership of any assets. We all wish this were a smooth process, but more often than not fights between family members happen over who should get what.

In this case, the state decides how the deceased's property is passed to their heirs. If no heirs fit the state's formula, the assets may become the property of the state, meaning they keep your assets and auction them off to cash in on them. A will helps you avoid all of this and allows you to control the distribution of your assets and state your final wishes.

One other essential use of a will is that it allows you to recommend a guardian to care for your children or other dependent beneficiaries in the event of your death. When Pop Icon Michael Jackson died, he used a will to assign his mother, Katherine Jackson, as the guardian for his three minor children. If Katherine Jackson was unable or unwilling to serve as the children's guardian, then Diana Ross (yes, that Diana Ross) was named to serve as the backup guardian.

Because the responsibility of taking care of a child can be overwhelming, you should select your guardian(s) carefully and get their permission before you list them in your will. Ultimately, the final decision of guardianship will be made by the court, but the courts give a lot of weight to the parent's decision in the will.

You should also name the executor or administrator of your estate and how you would like that person to distribute your assets in your will. This should include how all your debts, taxes, and funeral expenses will be paid. A non-contestability clause will help you avoid family disputes. There is also a provision that says, if any beneficiary contests the will, his or her share becomes null and void. Choose using a non-contestability clause wisely; it's not suitable for every family's circumstance.

You can also use a trust to dictate EXACTLY how you want your funds to be distributed and used. The terms will and trust are often confused, but they are very different in a few ways.

A will which is actually short for last will and testament only goes into effect after the death of the testator (the person who wrote it). A living trust, on the other hand, goes into effect as soon as it is signed. You can change both a will and/or trust up until the time of your death; as long as you remain mentally competent. The exception to this rule is if you put into effect an irrevocable living trust, which is what the name implies; irrevocable, meaning it will last forever.

A trust is a legal arrangement where one person, called a "settlor" or "grantor," gives assets to another person (or an institution, such as a bank or law firm), called a "trustee." The trustee holds legal title to the assets for another person, called a "beneficiary." A living trust can govern and distribute any property it has been funded with. The person who created the trust transfers his/her assets into it after it is formed.

While any assets that are passed through a will require a probate court, assets in a trust do not require probate. The trust allows for control of how money can be spent because it can hold assets for the benefit of specific beneficiaries, such as minor children who cannot legally take ownership of their own property or any family member you feel would misuse their inheritances.

You can literally instruct the trust to only pay a certain amount over a certain period of time to avoid overspending and/or the depletion of the funds.

Wills also become a matter of public record when they're submitted to the court for probate. The terms of living trust remain private. Again, wills go into effect when you die while Trust can provide for you during life and death.

See steps below to begin the process of legacy building for you and your family

ACTIVITY #11 – LAUNCH YOUR FAMILY LEGACY PLAN

How to Make a Family Tree

The easiest way to draw a family tree is start with a family tree template (See below). Our family tree template starts you with a basic family structure but you can use it to build on. You'll want to decide what generation you want to start with. You can start with yourself and build backwards or start with an older generation like great grandparents and build downwards.

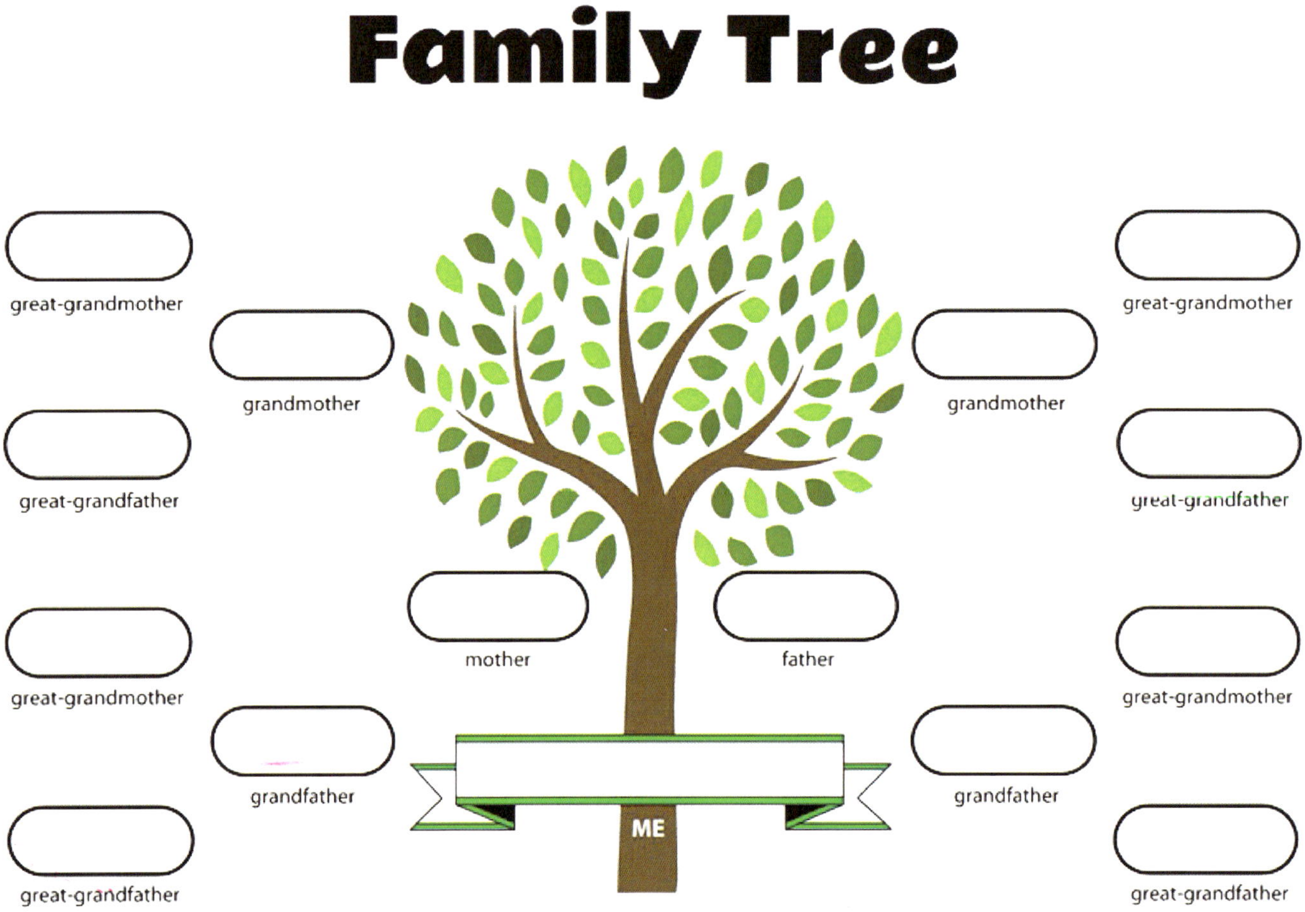

Action: Write your life Story

Buy a composition book and begin from the date you were born. Outline each year that something significant happened in your life up until today's date. Next to each significant date, write a brief summary of what happened. Now find someone your trust or hire someone from Fiverr or Upwork.com to interview you based on those dates you outlined. Transcribe the interview then edit it and add anything you are missing. After you story is written keep it in a safe place and write its location in your will so your family members can find it when needed. Going forward use and write a daily journal to keep your story fresh and update you book every 5-10 years

Action: How to Start on Your Estate Planning:

Now that you understand the importance of having a will. and/or trust. here's a list of steps that gives an overview of the estate planning process:

- Make a list of all your assets and liabilities.
- Purchase life insurance (If you didn't do so in step #7)
- Start a family discussion about who should be the guardian for your children.
- Check and update your current beneficiaries on your IRA. 401(K)'s. Life Insurance policies. etc.:
- Review the current estate tax exemption limits so you'll know how much you can transfer to heirs' tax-free.
- Determine how your money will be distributed upon your death (family. charity. etc.).
- Discuss your funeral arrangements with your spouse or family.
- Seek the assistance of a certified estate-planning attorney.

Keep in mind that direct transfers to your spouse are not taxed - these assets are not taxed until s/he dies (this is called a marital deduction).

Below are some Estate-Reduction and Planning Options

- Use trusts to maximize the exclusion and avoid probate. Trusts help you do so because they are designated to a beneficiary.
- Take advantage of charitable donations to reduce your estate.
- Use your estate to pay family educational and medical expenses as these are tax-deductible.
- Loan assets to family members to minimize your estate.
- Buy life insurance to help pay estate taxes, but remember life insurance will provide payouts only under certain conditions (executor or beneficiary should be the owner).
- Utilize annual gifting to minimize taxes and maximize the value to your loved ones on your will.
- Set up durable powers of attorney.
- Establish your funeral and burial plans.

Make sure you get professional help from your financial advisor. an estate-planning specialist. or a lawyer specializing in estates.

"Don't be a VICTIM of negative self-talk - remember YOU are listening."

- Bob Proctor

Changing Your Money Language

The importance of having a positive mental attitude can be summed up in three words: Law of Attraction! For years people have studied this law, concluding that a person's thoughts, emotions, and beliefs attract their experience; or simply "you get what you think about most."

In my lifetime, I've read plenty of books that focus on the law of attraction which include Think and Grow Rich, The Secret, As a man thinketh, Mr. Everit's Secret and many others. Understanding the law of attraction is a critical step in creating financial freedom; even though a lot of us don't truly recognize its power.

If you take a moment and think, you will realize that your attitude towards something is the reason whether good or bad, why you are in a particular situation. Think back to anything you've accomplished in your life; I guarantee that at that moment, you were in the right frame of mind, which in turn attracted it to you.

Think about all the things you didn't get; I can also guarantee that in some way you were thinking negatively, which in turn created that reality as well. When I say negatively, it can mean different things. Worry, anxiety, stress, fear, etc.; are all negative feelings that will not create wealth, nor will it help you obtain any goal or aspiration.

There is a saying "the rich get richer and the poor stay poor," most of this has to do with their attitudes. Rich people are rich because they know what it is to live life abundantly, so the fear of not having isn't immediately present. The absence of this fear allows rich people to concentrate on accumulating more wealth; hence, the term the rich get richer.

On the other hand, the poor only know to be poor, so any talk about no longer having to struggle is not a reality to them. Because of this, they concentrate on just sustaining life; they live life as it comes and don't have a real expectation of living life abundantly. The poor have an attitude of expecting the worst and hoping for the best. This expectation of the worst is what prolongs misfortune and guarantees that their situation stays constant.

Obtaining financial freedom is simple: If you want to change your life, you have to change your mind! You must have an unwavering belief in yourself and your ability and do what your heart desires because there are no ceilings! Your circumstance does not define you; its how you respond to them that makes the difference.

You can either be happy or be miserable; the work is all the same! Staying in good spirits is vital because what you resist will persist and what you focus on will continue to be part of your reality.

To begin to attract the life that you deserve, you must first think positively and recondition your mind. Your thoughts create your reality, so without changing your mind, it will be challenging to change your life. Contrary to popular belief, life is easy, and most of the things that fear teach us to worry about hardly ever do happen. Those who try too hard never really obtain true riches and financial freedom. Their eagerness to be successful transcends into anxiety, impatience, and fear, which are all negative feelings that can never bring abundance.

ACTIVITY #12 – MAINTAIN A POSITIVE MONEY MINDSET & LANGUAGE

Practicing the following steps will ensure that you look at life the way you were supposed to and begin the process of financial freedom.

1. **Improve Your Surroundings:** You must immediately rid yourself of anything in your life that is negative. This includes the type of movies you watch, the music you listen to, and the people you interact with daily. As a general rule: If it doesn't make you feel good, you shouldn't be doing it!

   Action: Create a list of things that make you feel good. For example: a walk in the park, playing your favorite sport, spending time with your loved ones, etc.; after you have compiled your list, include at least one of these activities in your weekly schedule. If your schedule permits do more than one, but one item is the minimum.

2. **Be Grateful:** Gratitude is one of the best ways to keep a positive attitude. A negative mindset can stem from greed, self-pity, jealousy, and not being fully satisfied with what you have now. If you get into the "attitude of gratitude," you will immediately rid yourself of most negative thoughts because you will realize that the things you need in life are already yours. When you're grateful, you begin to think about the less fortunate and realize how you don't really have it that bad. People complain about not having enough money to buy new shoes, but what about those folks who have no feet!! You may have thought I was going to say "no shoes," but I took it a step further to show how being grateful to have feet has now diminished the importance of a new pair of shoes. Be grateful for the little things, and the bigger things will come easily. Give thanks that you woke up this morning, give thanks that you can do what you need to, to change your life and give thanks that you are you.

   Action: Create a gratitude list which includes all of the things that you are grateful for. Things we often take for granted like family, friends, employment, shelter, clothes, neighbors, education, food, health, freedom, etc.; as you go through your day remind yourself as often as needed what you are grateful for. Make it a habit to give thanks every morning before you leave the house.

3. **Look at the bigger picture:** Often, we allow the small things that go wrong to take precedence over the more important things. You must keep your goal in your mind's eye so that the little things won't have such a significant effect on your ultimate goal. I had a teacher who once told me, "Don't lose the forest, for the tree." At first, I didn't understand the significance of that statement, but now I realize that that was the best advice someone has ever given me. When you concentrate so much on the small things and give so much negative energy towards it, you jeopardize losing it all and sacrificing all that you have worked hard for.

4. **Create Positive Self-Talk:** Creating positive self-talk is the process of eliminating yourself from negative thoughts. Words like I can't, I'll try, I hope, I wish, are all defeating words that need to be removed from your vocabulary immediately. Self-Confidence is having full faith in your abilities no matter what and knowing that anything is possible. You must begin the process of telling yourself positive things enough times that it will eventually seep into your subconscious. This method is what most people know as autosuggestion. When you begin to tell yourself positive things, you begin to get rid of all of the negative things that were in your mind and create a positive reality. Lack of confidence is a disease, and you must positively talk to yourself and convince yourself that you can become the person that you want to be. Negatively, it is known that if you tell a lie long enough, you begin to start to believe that lie. Creating positive self-talk is using that theory positively to build self-confidence.

   Action: Repeat the following affirmations to yourself every night before you go to sleep:

   I know that what I think about the most whether positive or negative will eventually come true, so I will think of myself positively and concentrate all of my thoughts daily on the person I want to be and lifestyle I want to live.

I deserve to be happy and successful and now have committed myself, my thoughts, and my actions towards this goal and will do whatever it takes to make it so.

I know that I have what it takes to achieve my long and short-term goals. Nothing can stop me! I will stop making excuses and use any obstacles as the fuel I need to keep going.

I have the power to change myself. I will no longer blame others for my circumstances. I will do whatever it takes to turn all of my dreams into reality.

I have full faith in my abilities and trust that by doing my best; I can accomplish any task, no matter how big or small. Impossible is nothing! I vow to do my best in everything I do and will never stop trying until I achieve it.

I know that no type of wealth, money, or position will last long if it's not gained through truth and justice. I promise to never indulge in any schemes, scams, cons, or any business deal that does not have a positive effect on everyone involved.

By repeating these affirmations every day, I will attract good people and circumstances to bring me closer to my goal. I will eliminate all negative thoughts and feelings. I will no longer feel hatred, envy, jealousy, or selfishness towards anyone. I know that to help others is to help myself, so I will also be of assistance to others and help them in the pursuit of their goals.

5. **Faith it til you make it:** A lack of confidence usually stems from self-doubt. Most people give themselves less credit then they deserve by allowing other people's experiences and failures to dictate what they are capable of doing. Faith it til you make it, is the last step in building self-confidence and will give you the courage you need to fully become who you want to be. For so long we were told by friends, family, and society what we can and can't do that we began to believe these limitations. Our belief in these restrictions caused us to doubt many things that we were ready for and capable of doing. "Faith it til you make it" which simply means to become the person you want to be well before you have obtained the status, is the process of proving to yourself that those "limitations" are nonexistent and confirms the FACT that thoughts become things. It is no coincidence that the people who are prosperous in life are the ones who take the initiative, do more than they are paid to do, and vividly keep their success in their mind's eye. "Faith it til you make it, is simply giving you the power to do the same!

Action: Create a personal statement of what your ultimate goal in life is. Write down every single detail of what you would like to accomplish, and then write it as if you have attained it already.

For example, My Personal Statement goes as such:

I am happy that I am financially free. I have gained my wealth in various amounts and in various ways.

I am a bestselling author who has written several books that have sold millions of copies. I have sold these copies by providing the best possible book that helps and empowers anyone who reads it.

I am a film producer who created video series that helped shed light on social and financial issues that have been seen millions of times.

I am a highly sought after paid speaker who receives thousands of dollars per talk. People come and hear me speak over and over, each time touching their hearts and moving them into action.

I am an Emmy Award-winning Talk Show host as well as a Radio personality on a nationally syndicated show. Collectively both shows attract millions of viewers and listeners and have created a dialogue for Self-Improvement.

I created motivational albums that have sold millions of copies via compact disc, mp3's and all other forms of digital format.

I am successful and still have time to spend with my family. I have a perfect work/life balance and a beautiful relationship with my wife and kids. My family and friends are proud of me and I help each of them fulfill their dreams.

All of my ventures provide jobs and entrepreneurial opportunities for all of the people I care for.

I believe in myself and in my abilities, with no restrictions and will continue to live life to its fullest.

As per the example above, your personal statement must be specific and include your definite purpose in life. You must list how you expect to obtain it and what you intend to give back. Begin at once to become the person you want to be; you must walk like it, talk like it, breathe like it, dress like it, think like it. Become It!! Every morning when you wake up, you must repeat your personal statement aloud while looking in the mirror and again before you go to sleep. As you go out into the world remember who that person is and begin to be that person immediately. As time goes on you will subconsciously start to visualize yourself being that person and as a person thinketh so shall they be!

WARNING! What isn't "Faith it til you make it"? Some people pretend to live a lifestyle that they cannot afford. They don't have their priorities in order and spend money trying to impress others. Playing act forces one to have to keep up an image that is not really them; this requires too much energy, wastes money, and doesn't help begin the habit of accumulation. "Faith it til you make it' should only be used in conjunction with your personal statement. Any other use will be counter-productive to financial freedom.

Affirmations have been one of the best things that I have done to change my life for the better.

It doesn't matter what other people say to you; it is what you say to yourself that matters most. In the beginning, you may feel like affirmations don't work or you are lying to yourself, but eventually, if you stick to them, they will start to change your belief system for the better.

Money & Wealth is a Mindset

Below are a set of affirmations that I want you to recite aloud at least once per day:

I Am a Multi-Millionaire!

I Have a Millionaire Mind!

Everyday in Every Way, I Am Getting Better and Better!

I Love Myself, Unconditionally!

I Am Building a Financially Stable Future for Myself and My Family!

Success and wealth Comes to me, Effortlessly!

I Am Willing to Accept the Best That Life Has to Offer!

I Am a Great Provider for My Family!

I Am Proud of My Contribution to the World!

I Appreciate ALL That I Have!

I Always Do My Best!

My Dreams Are Coming True!

I Manage My Money Wisely!

I Focus on My Goals!

My Self-Worth and Net Worth are Building Every Day!

I Believe in Unlimited Possibilities!

Get into the habit of reciting affirmations so you can believe in yourself and your power more. w

My friend Latisha Styles, founder of Creating Coins and President of Financial Success Media, LLC posted this great affirmation on her Facebook page, that I now use almost daily:

I receive as a result of my energy, expectation, and vibration.

I am worthy to receive.

There's nothing I need to do.

I simply need to be.

I receive just because I am me.

I am fearfully and wonderfully made.

When I get distracted by what others are doing, and I feel anxious and ask myself, "What should I do?"...

...I quickly rephrase and instead ask myself, "Who should I be?"

The answer comes from a small still voice saying, "Just be you."

Then I know exactly what actions to take, or if I should just sit, or who I should reach out to.

And things continue to manifest with each emotion-filled thought.

My version of a #LavishLife continues to unfold, and I am being surprised and delighted every step of the way. #OpentoReceive

Note: I use this anytime my energy starts to drift, or I start thinking less of myself for whatever reasons

Additional Forms And Resources

YOUR PERSONAL FINANCIAL WEBSITE

A Guide to Getting Started

MINDRIGHT
MONEY MANAGEMENT

Manage your wealth *and* your well-being

Your Personal Financial Website helps you see your financial life beyond the numbers. And with our automated fact finding questionnaire, you can get started with your Personal Financial Website on your own in just a few easy steps.

STEP 1

Register for your financial website

Click the link sent to your inbox to get started.
Then, create your own secure user name and password.

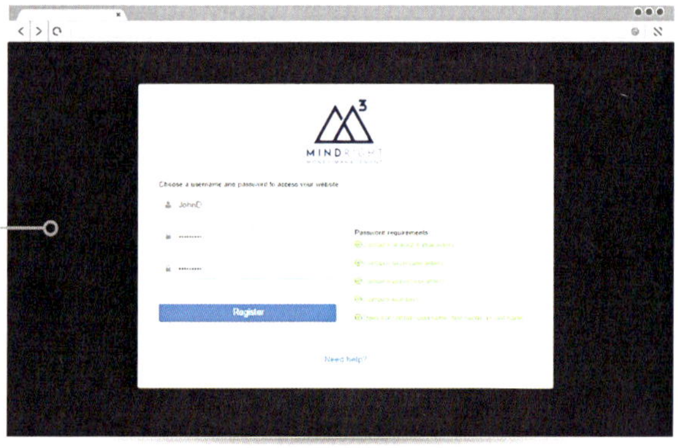

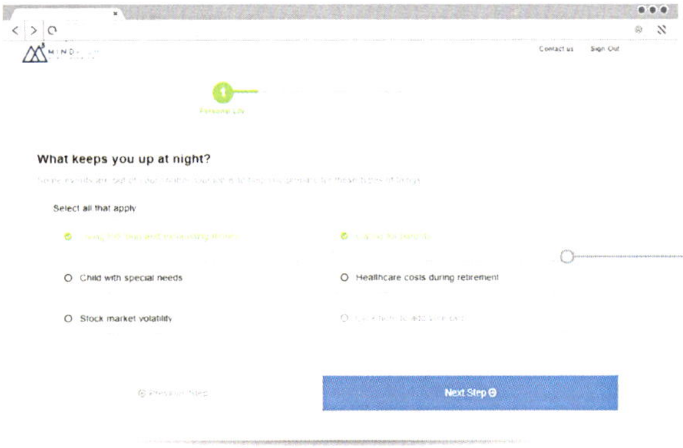

STEP 2

Complete the series of introductory questions

Answer a few basic questions to help us understand your current finances and future goals.

STEP 3

Connect your financial accounts

From your Homepage, click on Organizer, then Accounts to start adding your financial institutions, like bank and credit accounts.

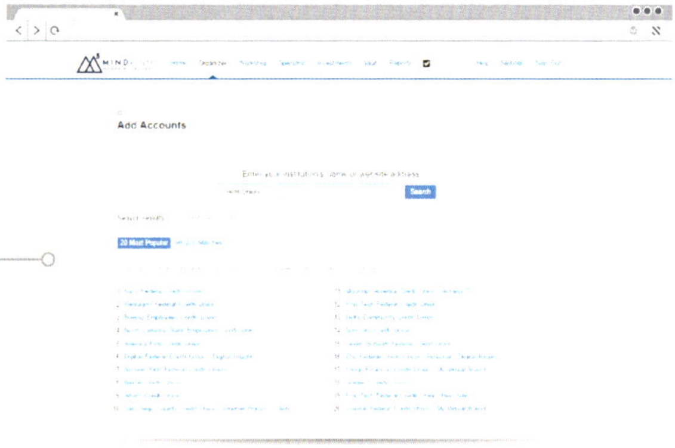

MINDRIGHT
MONEY MANAGEMENT

MINDRIGHT
MONEY MANAGEMENT

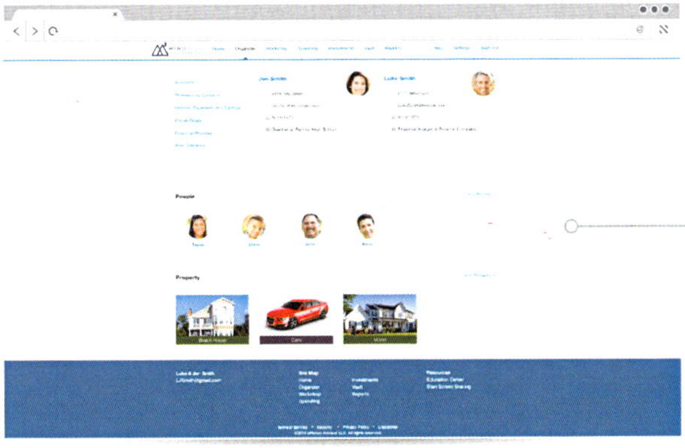

STEP 4
Personalize your website

Customize your website by adding photos of what your wealth represents—the people and things most important in your life.

STEP 5
See your finances come to life

Easily organize and track your financial goals with spending and budgeting tools, investment monitoring, and more.

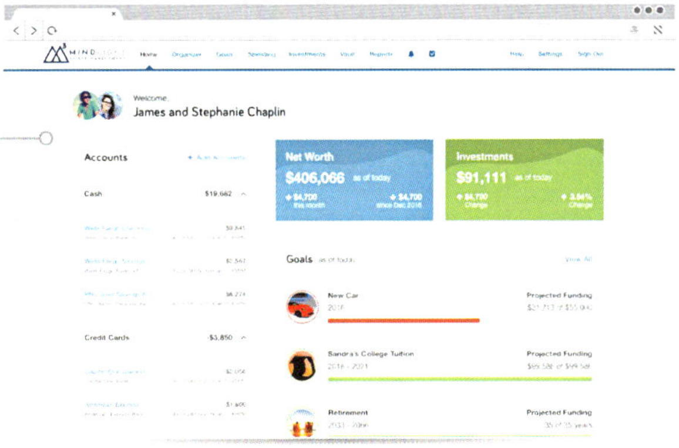

Now you're ready to start managing your wealth with your personal financial website!

By combining our personal digital experience with the professional guidance only a trusted advisor can provide, we can work together to build and monitor a financial plan that fits your needs.

MINDRIGHT
MONEY MANAGEMENT

YOUR PERSONAL FINANCIAL WEBSITE

MINDRIGHT
MONEY MANAGEMENT

Take Control of Your Financial World

Your Personal Financial Management website makes it easy to manage both your wealth and your well-being.

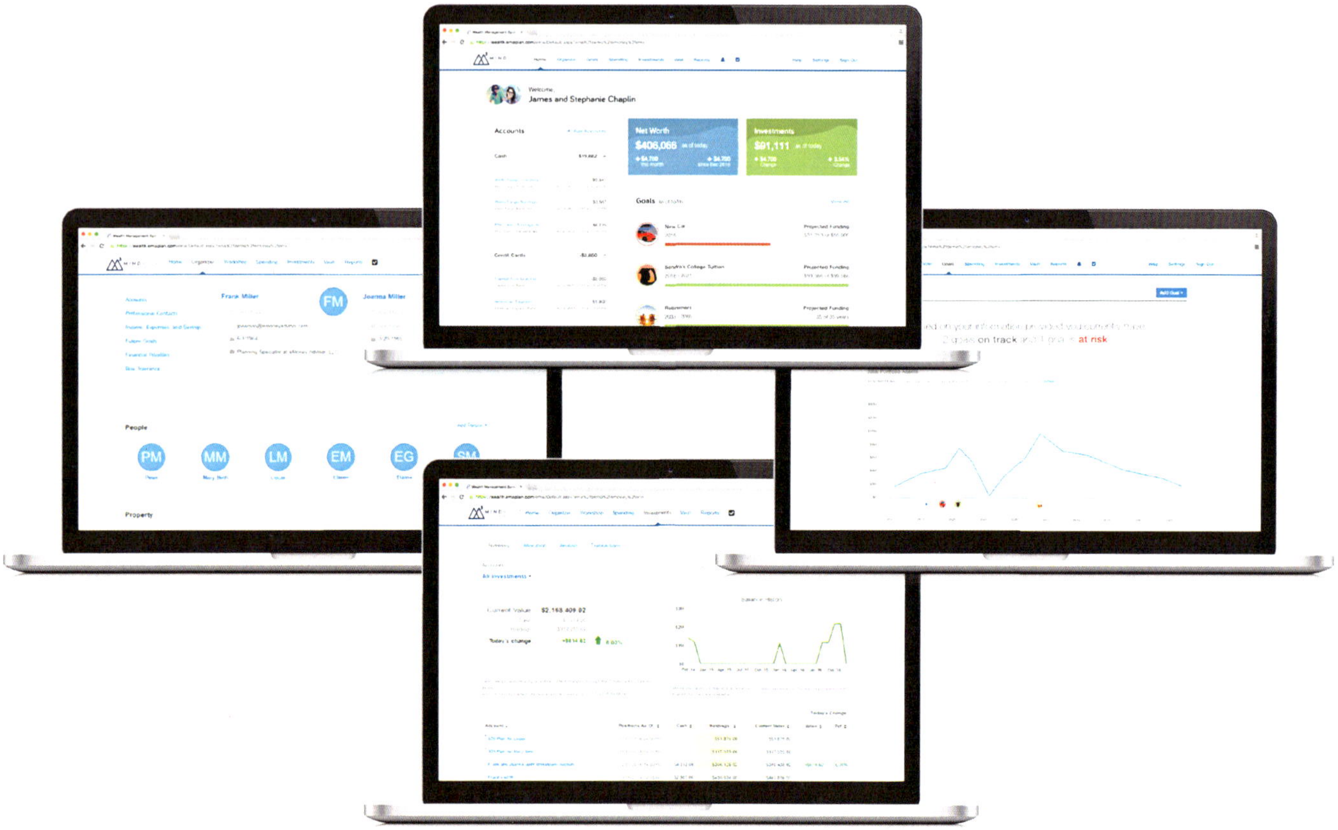

Organize. Monitor. Collaborate.

ORGANIZER
Connect all your accounts for a consolidated view of your entire financial picture.

INVESTMENTS
Interactive charts and detailed views help monitor all your accounts.

SCREEN SHARING
Join a screen sharing session quickly and easily for interactive planning anytime, anywhere.

VAULT
Safely store your most important financial documents, accessible 24/7.

TRACK SPENDING
Know how much you're spending, and where.

BUDGETING TOOLS
Set budgets to help reach your savings goals.

MOBILE
A complete financial picture available on your smart phone.

GOALS
See if you're on target to reach your most important goals.

MINDRIGHT
MONEY MANAGEMENT

YOUR PERSONAL FINANCIAL WEBSITE

MINDRIGHT MONEY MANAGEMENT

See the Big Picture

Connect Your Accounts to See Your Financial Snapshot

See a complete picture of your financial well-being updated automatically, every day. Get started by adding your financial accounts, like your checking account or retirement account, to your Personal Financial Website.

TO ADD A CONNECTION, FOLLOW THE STEPS BELOW:

- Log into your Personal Financial Website
- Click ***Add Account***
- Select ***I have an online login to this account***
- Type the name of the institution into the search bar
- Choose the connection from the list
- Enter your username and password

Once you've connected your accounts, see your financial scenario come to life!

KEEP THESE TIPS IN MIND WHEN ADDING AND MANAGING YOUR CONNECTIONS:

1. Test your credentials. Before entering your username and password in your Personal Financial Website, log into your financial institution to ensure your credentials are up-to-date.
2. Be proactive. If you make any changes to your account, like setting a new password, be sure to update your credentials in your Personal Financial Website too.

Having trouble with a connection?

Connections may break occasionally. If you run into a Connections error, try these steps or contact your advisor for help.

Click on *Find New* to begin. This starts a new session at your financial institution, ensuring you are troubleshooting the most recent error that may be affecting your connection.

Re-enter log-in credentials. Some financial institutions set passwords to expire after a certain length of time. If this happens, you'll need to update your password at your financial institution and then update the connection on your Personal Financial Website.

One-time access code. Some financial institutions require a secure access code before connecting to your Personal Financial Website, which will be sent from your bank via email, text, or phone call. If you see this error, be sure to log in at the institution's website directly before requesting the access code be sent.

Do not delete the account. Deleting the connection will remove any accounts, transaction history, and tickets that are currently open. This can affect your spending and budgets and delay our ability to resolve the issue.

MINDRIGHT MONEY MANAGEMENT

Stay Aware with Alerts

Your Personal Financial Website allows you to create a custom set of alerts that notify you of important dates, reminders, and account and investment changes.

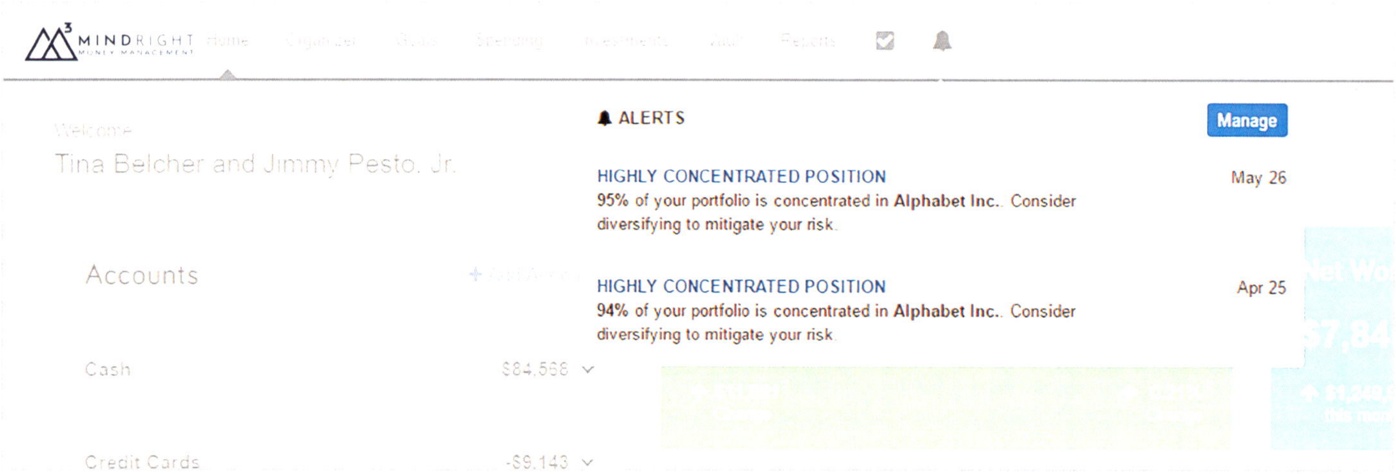

WHEREVER YOU GO

Whether via email or on the home screen of your Mobile Personal Financial Website, alerts help you stay in-the-know, wherever you go.

MONITOR SECURITY

Alerts for high credit balance, large expenses, and budget exceeded allow you to respond quickly to unusual account activity.

AVOID FEES

Save money by being alerted to low cash balances and unexpected bank fees.

ALWAYS REMEMBER

Be reminded of upcoming events like birthdays and anniversaries. Also be alerted to important financial dates like social security benefits, required minimum distributions, and tax filing dates.

SET UP YOUR ALERTS NOW!

1. Log on to your Personal Financial Website.
2. Click on Manage in the bell icon on the navigation bar, or click on Settings in the top right corner of your Home Page.
3. Your email address is already added for you to receive email alerts. You can add additional Email Recipients too.
4. Turn on the Alerts you prefer and set the criteria for each.

MINDRIGHT
MONEY MANAGEMENT

Spending

Are your daily spending habits helping you meet your long-term financial objectives? With the Spending tab in your Personal Financial Website you can easily monitor and manage your daily cash flow — helping you stay on track to meet the financial future that you envision.

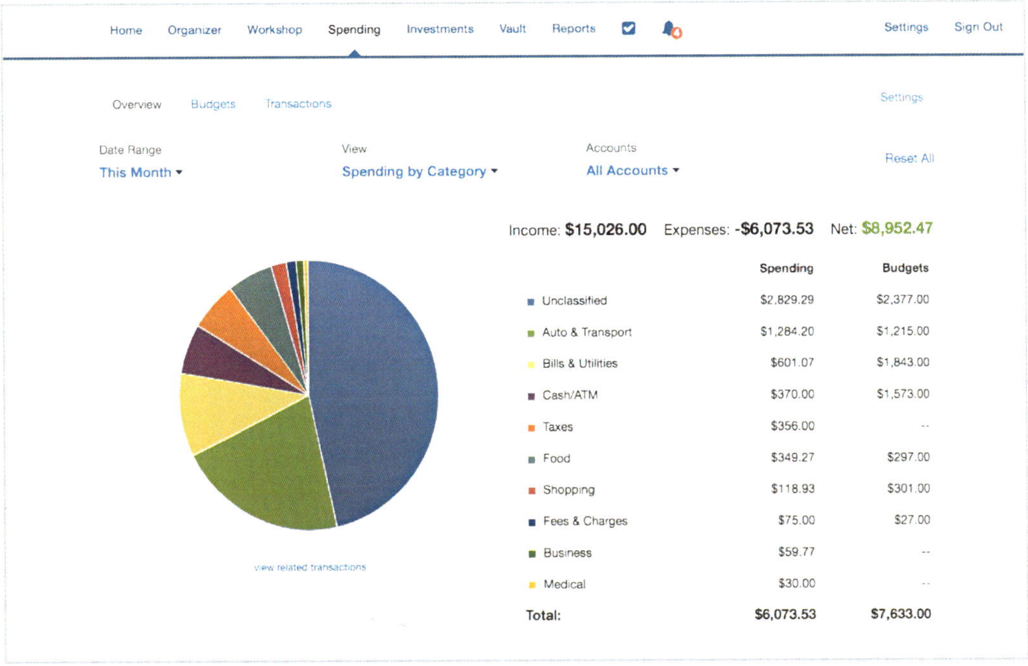

VISIBILITY INTO ALL ACCOUNTS

Connecting all your financial accounts brings your daily transactions from multiple institutions into one place for a complete and consolidated view of your spending.

REAL-TIME EXPENSE TRACKING

Your daily spending transactions will instantly update in the Spending tab once you've connected your financial accounts. With a real-time view of all your debits and credits, you'll always know how much you've spent and what's left.

INSIGHT INTO SPENDING HABITS

Financial transactions are automatically classified based on preset and customizable categories. You'll easily identify where you spend the most money and ways to save for future expenses.

BUDGETING IN ONE-CLICK

Getting started with planning for your future income and expenses is simple. In just one-click, create a budget from your actual spending transaction history. Use this budget as is or as a starting point that you can easily customize.

MINDRIGHT
MONEY MANAGEMENT

Interactive Cash-Flow Planning

THE DECISION CENTER

Planning for the future can feel like an overwhelming concept – but with financial advice and technology backing your decisions, it doesn't have to be.

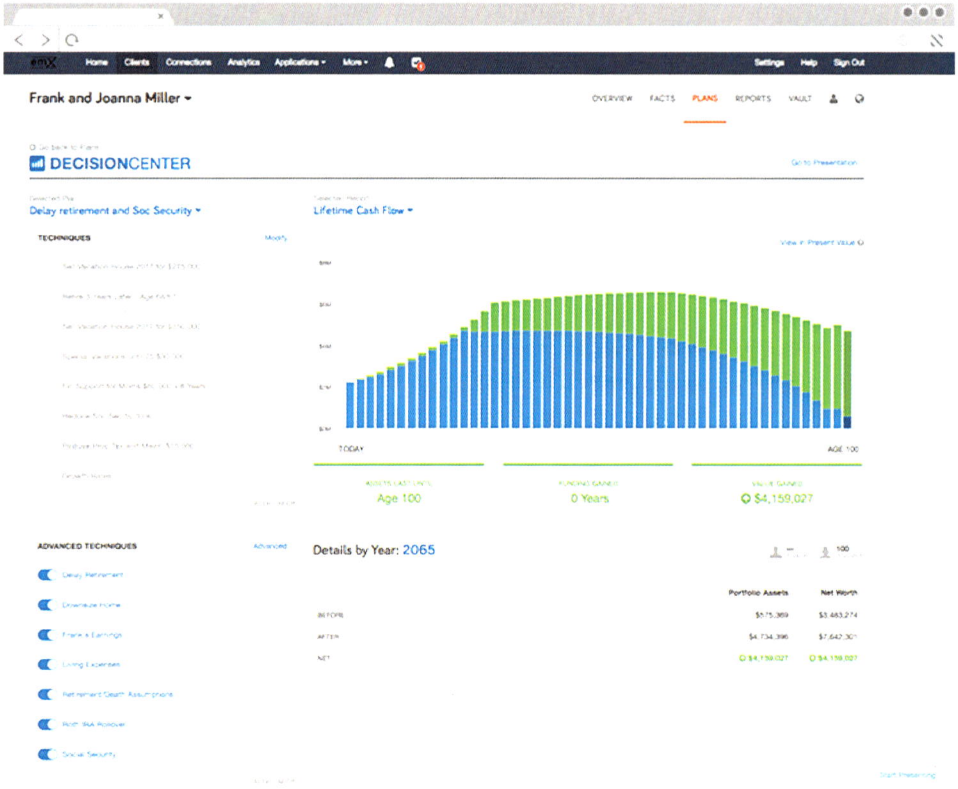

PRIORITIZE YOUR GOALS

We'll work together to evaluate your goals and create a custom plan focused on helping you reach them. And because life is always changing, your plan should be dynamic as well.

SEE FUTURE PROJECTIONS

You'll be able to see the projected impact of your financial decisions on your goals in real-time so you can visualize how each piece of your financial puzzle fits together.

SIMULATE MULTIPLE SCENARIOS

We'll explore what-if scenarios to help you understand how potential changes may impact your goals, giving you the insight you need to make more informed decisions about your financial future.

Visualize your financial plan with our interactive Decision Center.

Investments

Keeping track of all your investment accounts can be cumbersome when they are held at multiple financial institutions. The Investments section of your Personal Financial Website gives you one place to view detailed summaries of all your financial accounts.

ACCOUNT VALUE HISTORY

Each month, your investment account balances are recorded so you can easily track if their value has increased or decreased over specific periods of time.

ASSET ALLOCATION

Easily view the asset types and holdings that make up your investment accounts so you always know how your assets are allocated.

CURRENT VALUES

Account holdings update with the market throughout the day so you always know the current value of your investments.

MARKET INSIGHTS

Easily access trusted market news and investment research from Morningstar so you can skip the online searches when you're interested in learning more about the markets.

Home Organizer Workshop Spending Investments Vault Reports Settings Sign Out

Summary Allocation Analysis Transactions Research

Accounts

All Investments ▾

All Asset Types

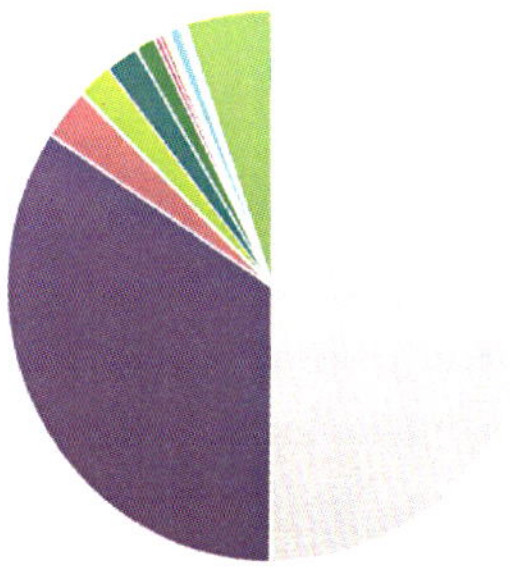

	Value	% of Type	% of Portfolio
Equities			
Balanced	$2,235,094.29	53.50%	50.11%
Large-Cap Blend	$1,525,404.11	36.51%	34.20%
Small-Cap Growth	$134,473.11	3.22%	3.01%
Large-Cap Value	$93,691.03	2.24%	2.10%
Large-Cap Growth	$91,014.14	2.18%	2.04%
Mid-Cap Value	$55,101.64	1.32%	1.24%
International	$16,115.14	0.39%	0.36%
Mid-Cap Blend	$12,398.28	0.30%	0.28%
Mid-Cap Growth	$8,968.11	0.21%	0.20%
Emerging Markets	$3,537.24	0.08%	0.08%
Small-Cap Value	$1,071.95	0.03%	0.02%
Small-Cap Blend	$1,033.09	0.02%	0.02%
Subtotal	**$4,177,902.13**		**93.67%**

MINDRIGHT
MONEY MANAGEMENT

Visualize the Impact of Every Recommendation

With Interactive Planning technology, we won't tell you how your decisions will affect your financial future, we'll show you.

GOALPLANNER
Interactive Goal-Based Planning

Probability of Success

Define goals and track your progress towards them.

DECISIONCENTER
Interactive Cash Flow Planning

Visualize the impact of goals and recommendations in real-time.

DISTRIBUTIONCENTER
Interactive Estate Planning

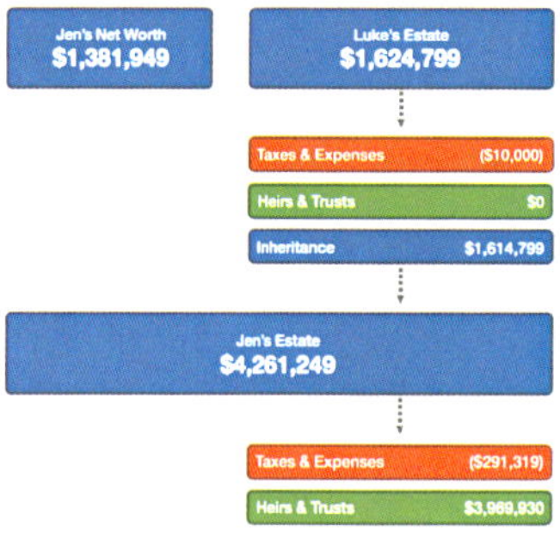

Leave a lasting legacy to those most important to you.

Find real-time answers to your questions – both in person and online. After all, it's your financial plan – **that's why we build it together**.

MINDRIGHT
MONEY MANAGEMENT

YOUR PERSONAL FINANCIAL WEBSITE

MINDRIGHT
MONEY MANAGEMENT

Leaving a Legacy

THE DISTRIBUTION CENTER

See a personalized story of your estate with the Distribution Center.

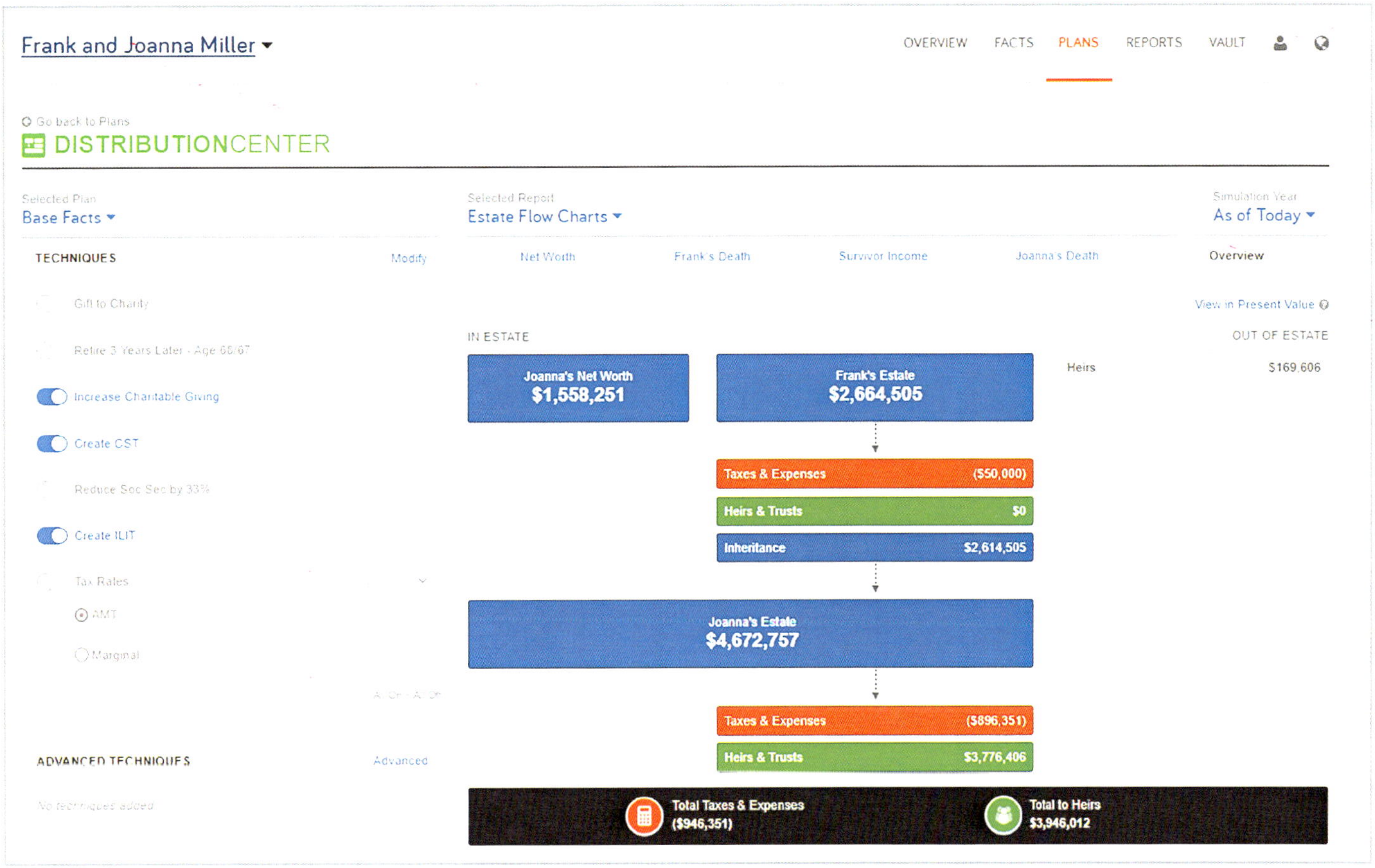

REVIEW OPTIONS TOGETHER

We'll assess the risks and benefits of estate planning scenarios and work with you to better protect your legacy.

SEE PROJECTIONS IN REAL-TIME

Make live adjustments to your estate plan to project the possible impact of your financial decisions.

VISUALIZE YOUR ESTATE PLAN

See the effects of multiple estate planning techniques, like trusts or charitable giving.

With the interactive Distribution Center, you can be sure you're taking care of the people and organizations that matter most.

MINDRIGHT
MONEY MANAGEMENT

MINDRIGHT
MONEY MANAGEMENT

Safe & Secure

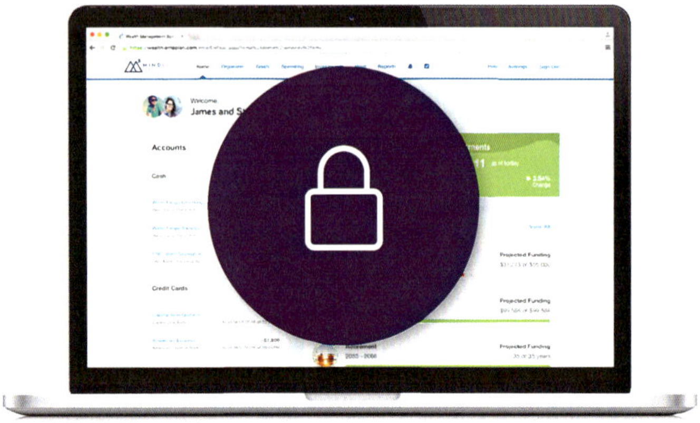

Your wealth management system employs advanced security features and protocols to keep your data safe, private, and secure at every hour of every day, year round.

Our comprehensive security measures include password protection, Secure Socket Layer encryption, firewalls, intrusion detection, audits, inspections, and more.

With each measure in place, you can be confident that your important information is safe and secure.

PASSWORD PROTECTION

You have a unique username and password, ensuring that only you can access your information. Submitting incorrect login credentials three consecutive times will automatically lock your account for 10 minutes. This is to block any manual or programmed hacking attempts.

In most cases, we have no access to your username or password. However, if you decide to provide us with this information, we will never share your username and password over the phone or send it to an email address not pre-registered with your account.

HIGHEST ENCRYPTION

Our system uses a 256-bit Secure Socket Layer to scramble your data, further preventing access to unauthorized users. This is the highest level of encryption currently available today, and twice the standard followed by many financial institutions, including banks.

SECURED DATA

We house your important data at secure, geographically separated data centers. Physical security measures at these facilities includes 24/x7/x365 on-site personnel and closed circuit video surveillance.

These data centers also make use of fire protection, electronic shielding, and database backup procedures to ensure your data is continuously monitored and protected.

ROUTINE SECURITY TESTING

Your wealth management system uses third-party security auditors and software, including TraceSecurity, Tenable Security and WhiteHat Security, to identify vulnerabilities within your system and to assist us with remediation efforts.

2-FACTOR AUTHENTICATION

Your wealth management system employs 2-Factor Authentication (2FA), a complete fraud detection platform that uses a dynamic risk- and rules-based approach to identify high-risk behaviors and initiate an additional layer of security. With 2FA, you are sent a verification code to your mobile phone, which you are required to input along with your username and password in order to access your personal financial website. This additional layer of protection safeguards your sensitive financial data and strengthens the security of your account by requiring two methods of verifying your identity.

NON-TRANSACTIONAL

Unlike online banking, trading or shopping websites, your money cannot be moved, withdrawn or accessed on our system.

MINDRIGHT
MONEY MANAGEMENT

MINDRIGHT
MONEY MANAGEMENT

Your Guide to Data Aggregation

WHAT IS DATA AGGREGATION?

Data aggregation is the process of gathering digital information – like your checking account, 401(k), and investment account balances – from a variety of separate sources, to combine the data into a unified set. Your Personal Financial Website uses Connections to aggregate your financial account information, allowing us to build a financial plan with all your information in mind.

WHAT IS SCREEN SCRAPING?

Screen scraping is a common method used in the data aggregation process, and refers to the collection and transfer of data from one application to another. In your Personal Financial Website, it requires you to submit your log-in credentials, which allows the site to "scrape" or copy financial data.

WHAT IS THE RISK OF SCREEN SCRAPING?

Screen scraping relies on you sharing your log-in credentials with your Personal Financial Website, which copies your data from your financial institution. While our technology company is held to stricter security standards than most, keeping your log-in credentials private is the safest way to protect your information.

WHAT IS AN API?

An API – or Application Program Interface – specifies how software components should interact with one another, which helps technology developers build more secure connections. APIs allow end-users to complete actions without having to go back and forth between two websites.

WHY ARE APIs MORE SECURE THAN SCREEN SCRAPING?

APIs offer a more secure way to collect and copy data because they do not require access to log-in credentials, which means no transactions can be made. Think of APIs as offering "view only" access to account data.

WHAT ARE OTHER BENEFITS OF USING APIs OVER SCREEN SCRAPING?

With traditional screen scraping methods, a client's access to their data may be disrupted by changes to their password, or changes an institution makes to its website, which may require screen scraping logic to be adjusted. By aggregating data through APIs, clients have more reliable access to their data as they are not impacted by institution changes like these.

WHAT CHANGES WILL BE MADE TO MY PERSONAL FINANCIAL WEBSITE?

While nothing is immediately changing, there will likely be minor action required in the future. For example, if you hold Fidelity accounts, you will eventually need to grant your Personal Financial Website access to your Fidelity account data through Fidelity Access™ — Fidelity's new method of sharing client data. We expect other institutions to announce similar methods in the future, so we'll be sure to keep you up-to-date on any action items.

MINDRIGHT
MONEY MANAGEMENT

Consumer Data Aggregation Checklist

MINDRIGHT
MONEY MANAGEMENT

Data aggregation is the process of gathering financial information and presenting it in a single comprehensive view. When it comes to your Personal Financial Website, that means connecting with and extracting information from the companies that manage your financial accounts and liabilities so that we can provide you with a consolidated view into your accounts in real-time.

The power of data aggregation lies in the fact that you gain a comprehensive view of your financial situation. Because it's important to protect your financial information, you should understand how a third party will access, store, and use your data before authorizing them to aggregate your data.

At MindRight Money Management™, we employ the industry's best practices in data security and privacy. Read on to learn how our data aggregation system works and how we stack up against recommendations from the Financial Industry Regulatory Authority's (FINRA) consumer guidelines.

FINRA: Weigh the benefits of aggregation against the risks of sharing your security credentials. Be particularly diligent when you authorize a third party to facilitate payments on your behalf. Check to ensure your payments go to the recipient.

We couldn't agree more with FINRA's guidance: It's important to understand the potential risk of sharing financial information with a third party. Your Personal Financial Website mitigates the risk by securely aggregating data so that we can develop informed financial plans.

Additionally, we do not facilitate payments of any kind on your behalf. In fact, you can use the Spending tab of the Client Portal to closely monitor and spot unauthorized transactions you might otherwise miss. When this feature is combined with notifications of specific transactions, you gain a single application through which you can monitor all of your accounts.

FINRA: Read the terms and conditions of any user agreement or contract you sign. Know what rights you are granting with respect to accessing your financial accounts and using your data. For instance, how often are your accounts scraped and what data is collected?

The Terms of Service (ToS) of your Personal Financial Website clearly and concisely outline our data aggregation procedures. These state that you are only granting access to your advisor so they can retrieve and view your account information.

FINRA: Understand the aggregator's privacy and data security measures. A good place to begin is by reading the aggregator's terms of use, privacy and security information. Here are some things to look for does (or may) the aggregator share your security credentials and data with, or provide access to your accounts to, another data aggregator or service provider? Does the aggregator sell your data to a third-party entity? If so, are you comfortable with that?

We only use client data for the benefit of the client and we do not and never will sell your data to a third-party entity.

FINRA: Does the aggregator use encryption when retrieving your data? How long is the data retained? What is the process of purging or disposing the data once you terminate your contract?

We fully encrypt production data while in transit. Highly sensitive data is encrypted at all times using AES 256-bit standard encryption - the same level of security as that used by most banks. Data is stored for your advisor's use until you end your relationship with the advisor or at your request.

FINRA: What happens if there is a data breach or any unauthorized access to your account? Is there a process in place to notify consumers and financial institutions should a breach occur?

Our provider has never had a security breach. However, we have implemented a robust security incident response plan should we suspect an issue. The plan includes identification, assessment, remediation, resolution, and notification. All company employees are trained to identify and properly report any suspected breach of confidential information.

FINRA: What type of liability, if any, does the aggregator bear in the event of a consumer loss due to a data breach or unauthorized access? Does the aggregator have the financial capacity or insurance coverage to compensate consumers for loss? Is there a dispute mechanism in place to resolve any issues related to data breaches or unauthorized access?

We follow standard aggregation industry best practices. Ultimately, the consumer is responsible for any damages due to unreported or unauthorized use of the consumer's login credentials.

FINRA: How accurate are the scraping algorithms used to collect data from your financial accounts? To find out, you can ask whether the aggregator conducts periodic checks to ensure that it is collecting data and using it accurately to provide the required service. You should also check the data yourself against your primary source accounts.

Our provider has a dedicated data support team staffed with experts and certified professionals whose goal is to ensure the functionality and accuracy of your data. At any time, we can open a ticket and have your connected accounts reviewed for accuracy.

FINRA: Check with financial data providers to find out what, if any, data is delivered to aggregators through an Application Programming Interface (API), which is generally considered a safer alternative than scraping.

While our current aggregation standards follow industry best practices, we are transitioning from screen scraping to an API-based approach to provide even greater peace of mind.

FINRA: Finally, make sure you cancel your account and terminate the access and rights you have granted to the aggregator once you discontinue using the service. Failing to do so may expose your financial information to ongoing security risks. Understand and follow the steps that need to be taken to stop the ability of the aggregator to access your account. This may involve more than just deleting the software application from your computer or mobile device.

We believe your data should always be secure and under your control. To that end, you can terminate your use of our service at any time. At your request, we will delete your account and purge your data from our system.

MINDRIGHT
MONEY MANAGEMENT

Answers in the Palm of Your Hand

With mobile access to your website, your complete financial picture is in the palm of your hand, whenever you want, from wherever you are.

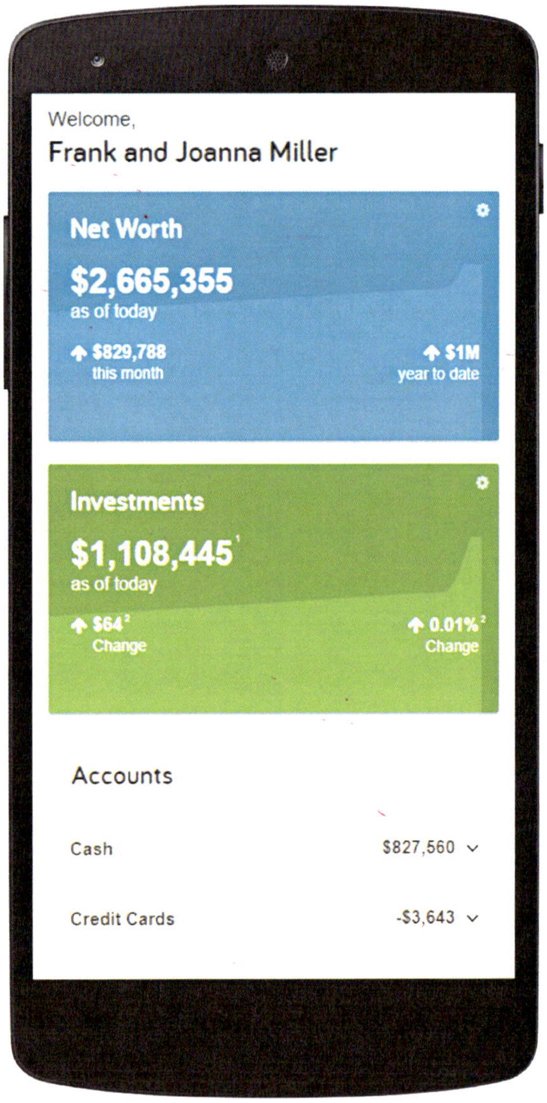

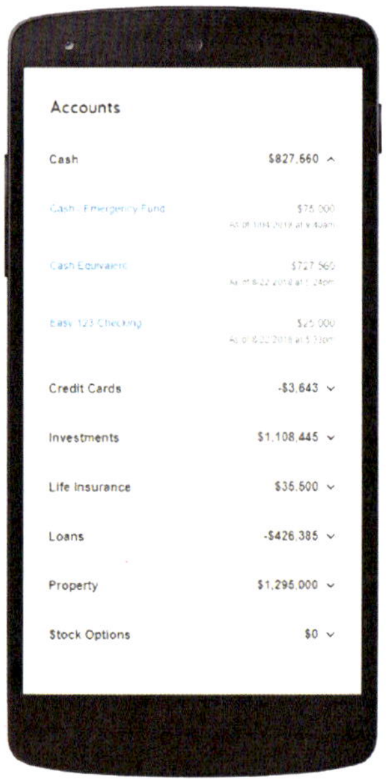

See All Your Accounts on One Page

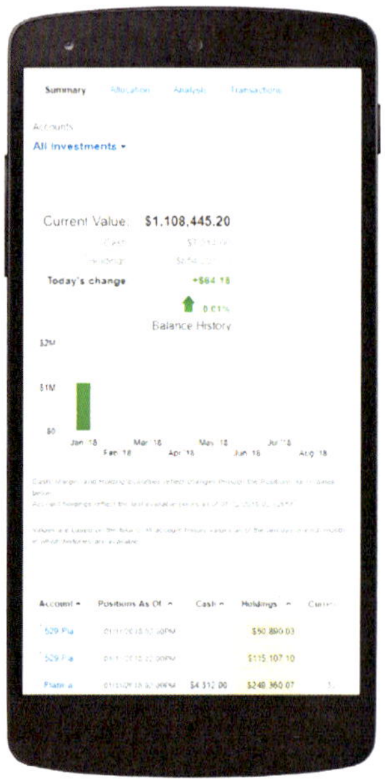

View Your Updated Investments

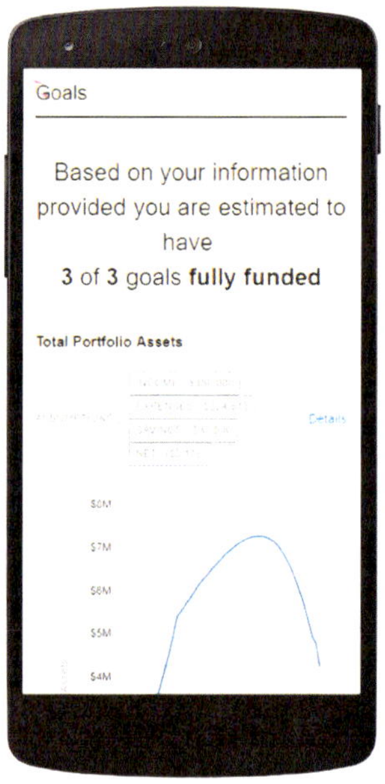

Track Your Progress Towards Your Goals

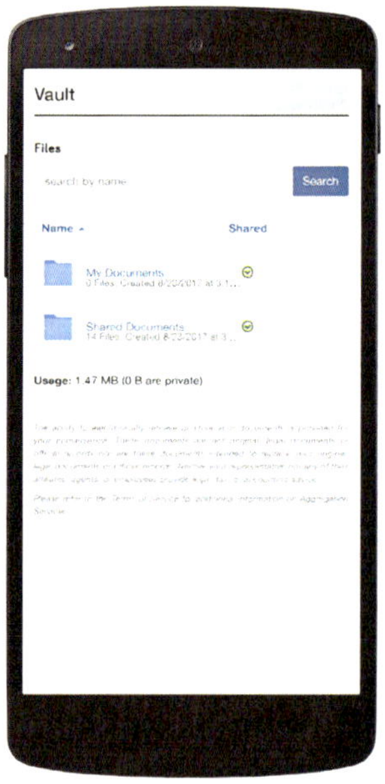

Access Important Documents

Your Personal Financial Mobile Website can be accessed on iPhone, Android, and other popular smart phones.

MINDRIGHT
MONEY MANAGEMENT

Here's How to Get Started

1. Once you've completed the self-registration process for your Personal Financial Website, you will receive a Website Registration Confirmation email.

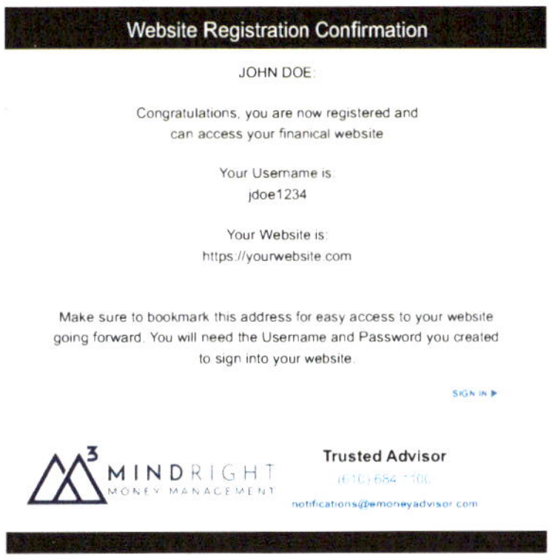

2. Using your smart phone, access your email and click on the URL provided. Before logging on, add or save the link to your smart phone's Home Screen.

3. The first time you log on, enter the same Username and Password you use to access your full Personal Financial Website. After this initial logon, you'll be prompted to register your device and create a 4 digit PIN for easier access in the future.

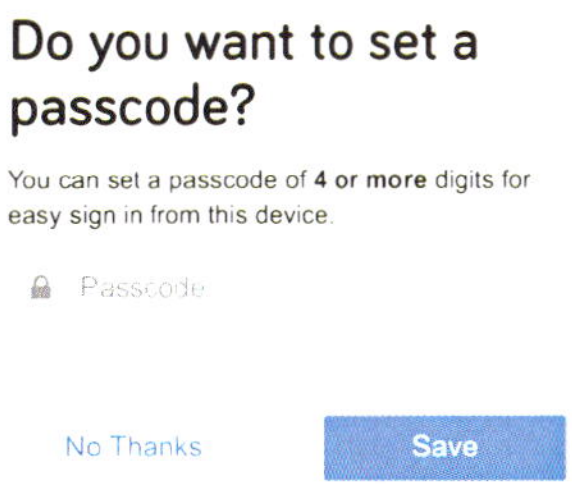

MINDRIGHT
MONEY MANAGEMENT

MINDRIGHT
MONEY MANAGEMENT

Best Practices for Using Your PFM Site

Your personal financial management (PFM) site offers a real-time, 24/7 view into your complete financial picture. As you are getting set up on your PFM, follow these tips to help you get the most out of this resource.

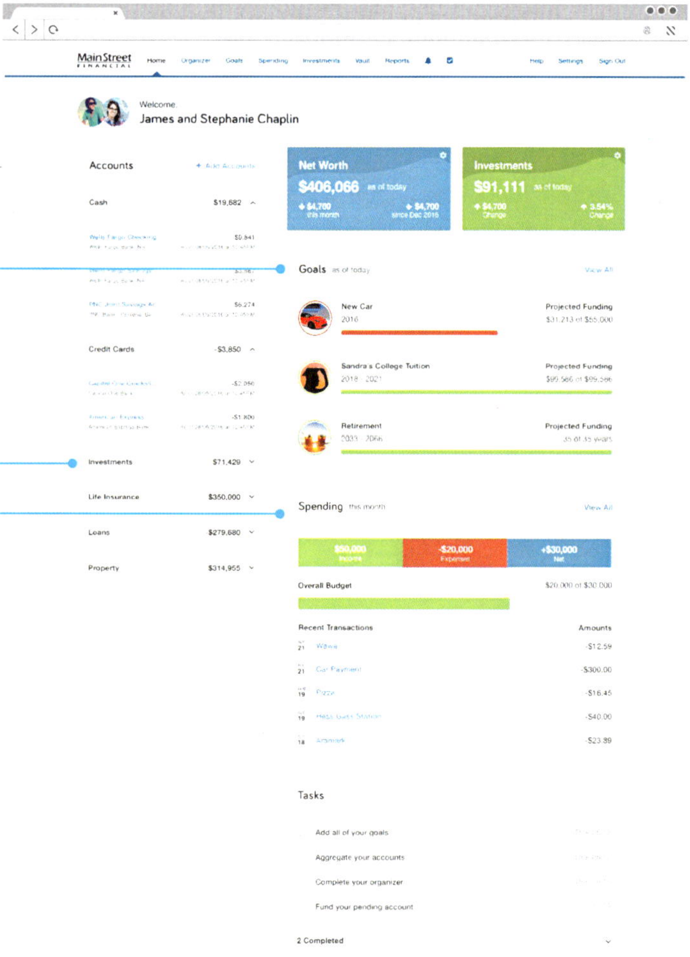

HOME SCREEN

Here you'll see a holistic picture of your financial health at a glance. The tiles on this page offer a snapshot into each section of the site, which you can drill down into for more information.

ORGANIZER

Consolidate all your important financial information in one place. Start by connecting your financial institutions in the "Accounts" section of the Organizer in order to get an updated view into your accounts and investments in real-time. Next, add in your goals and financial priorities and personalize your site by adding photos and important milestones.

GOALS

Easily add goals, track your progress toward funding those goals, and visualize how your goals impact your long-term financial outlook.

SPENDING

Access the Spending tab to see where your money is going each month, establish a budget to manage your expenses, and make adjustments based on actual spending, saving and investment data.

INVESTMENTS

Monitor your investment performance and asset allocation. Make sure to first connect all your investment accounts so you can get an accurate picture of your finances.

VAULT

Upload your important documents for safe keeping and easy access when you need them. Protected by the highest level of encryption in the industry, private folders provide a secure location to store sensitive files, while shared folders enable you and your advisor to easily share and access important documents for review.

MINDRIGHT
MONEY MANAGEMENT

MINDRIGHT
MONEY MANAGEMENT

Your Organizer

Connect your financial decisions to the people and things that matter most.

Organize.
Prioritize.
Personalize.

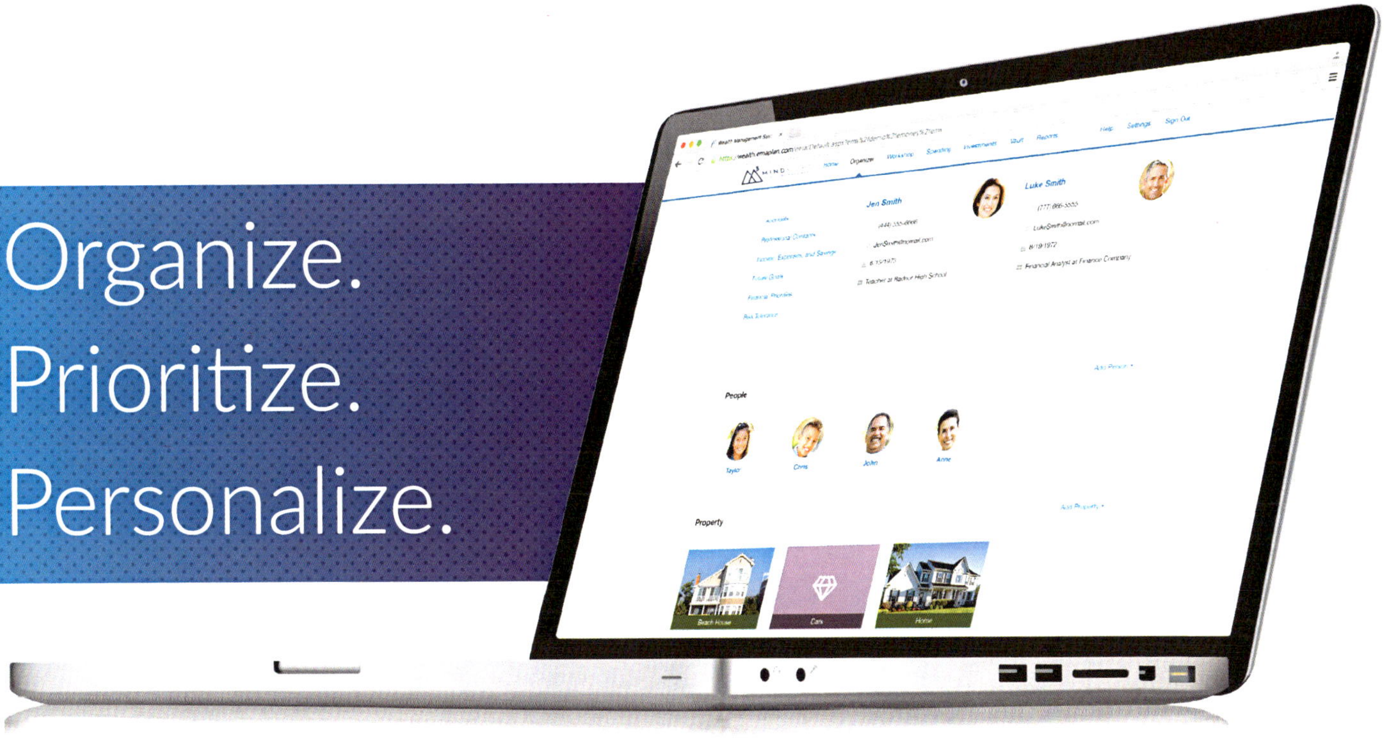

PEOPLE & PROPERTY

Personalize your Organizer to reflect the people and things that are most valuable to you.

ACCOUNTS

Connect all of your financial accounts to build a comprehensive picture of your financial life.

PROFESSIONAL CONTACTS

Store all your professional contacts in one place and access them from anywhere.

INCOME, EXPENSES & SAVINGS

See a breakdown of what you own, what you owe and how your savings are impacted.

FUTURE EXPENSES

Tell us what major expenses you expect to incur in the future and we'll help you build a plan to cover the anticipated costs.

FINANCIAL PRIORITIES

Prioritize your financial objectives and easily re-shift your focus as your goals change.

RISK TOLERANCE

Learn how much risk you're really comfortable taking in your investments.

MINDRIGHT
MONEY MANAGEMENT

YOUR PERSONAL FINANCIAL WEBSITE

The Goals Tab

Whether you're picturing life in retirement, saving for your child's education, or renovating your home, the best time to plan for it is today. With the interactive Goals tab of your Personal Financial website you can easily add your financial goals and track your progress toward funding those goals— from wherever you are, at any time.

PERSONALIZE YOUR GOALS

Add photos and timeframes to your goals to visualize the impact they have on your long-term financial outlook.

ESTIMATE PROJECTED FUNDING

Enter the details of your goals into your portal and gain insight into how you're tracking toward funding your goals and possible actions you can take to improve funding results.

DEDICATE FUNDS

If you already have saving accounts or funds set aside for a specific goal in mind, you can easily designate them as sources of funding for that goal to help you stay organized and on track.

STAY THE COURSE

With the ability to see your financial goals and projected funding results, you'll always know how you're tracking toward achieving your financial targets.

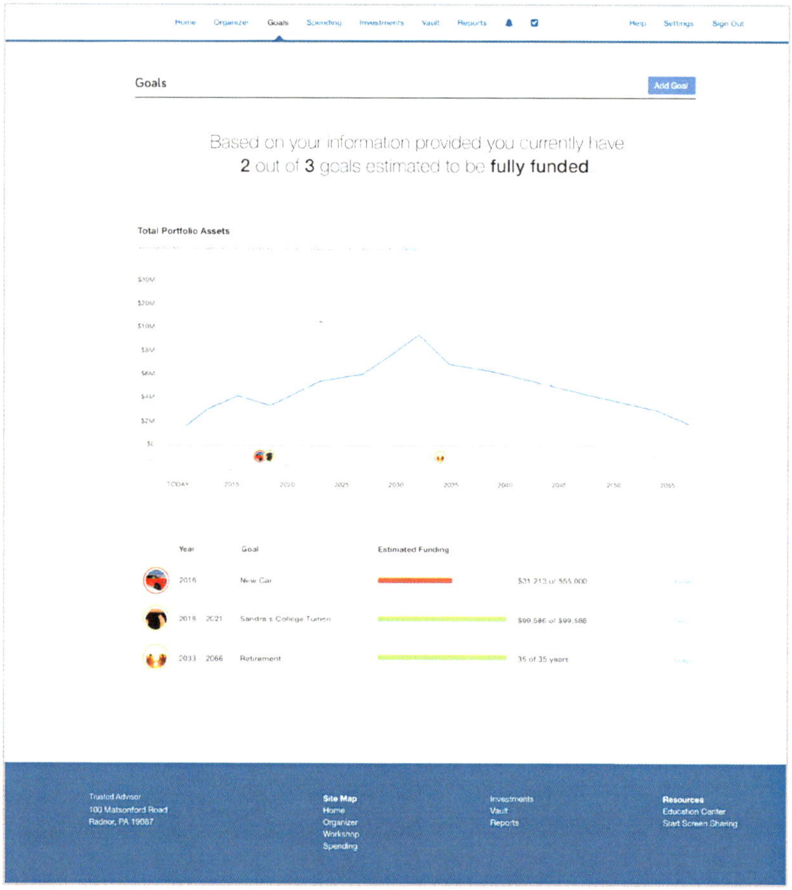

MINDRIGHT MONEY MANAGEMENT

MINDRIGHT
MONEY MANAGEMENT

Ready, Set, Goal!

Setting goals can be a tough task, but it is an important step toward securing your financial future. Before we create a financial plan, we'll work together to define and document your goals. Here's a primer to help you get started:

DETERMINE YOUR PRIORITIES

Think honestly about the life you envision for you and your loved ones. Don't just ask yourself what you are trying to achieve. Map out how you will get there. Be specific about these steps and record them as they are the basis for your goals.

BE REALISTIC

Set specific timeframes for accomplishing your goals. Ask yourself, "Can I actually accomplish this, or do I need to rethink things?"

TRACK YOUR PROGRESS

The Goals tab on your personal financial management site is a great tool to help you stay focused on your goals. You can add your goals, assign accounts to fund those goals, and monitor your progress toward reaching them.

MAKE ADJUSTMENTS BASED ON DATA

We'll work with you to model what-if scenarios and give you visibility into how small changes—such as delaying retirement or refinancing your home—can affect your goals.

ASK FOR HELP

When the unexpected occurs, your financial plan provides a foundation to make decisions. We can provide expert advice when you need it and refer back to your original goals to help you make informed decisions.

STICK WITH IT

Following a financial plan is an ongoing event. Your plan is the roadmap to help you achieve the financial future you envision for yourself. We'll work together to document your plan, refine it as needed, and help you stick to it and tax filing dates.

Remember, if you don't know how close or far away you are to reaching your financial goals, how will you ever get there? A plan will lead the way.

MINDRIGHT
MONEY MANAGEMENT

MINDRIGHT
MONEY MANAGEMENT

The Vault

At a moments notice, can you or your family members locate your most important files such as tax returns, wills, passports and birth certificates? With the Vault, you can. The Vault is a secure digital document storage repository. Using the Vault, you and your advisor can exchange confidential documents, collaborate on financial plans, and share personal data easily and securely.

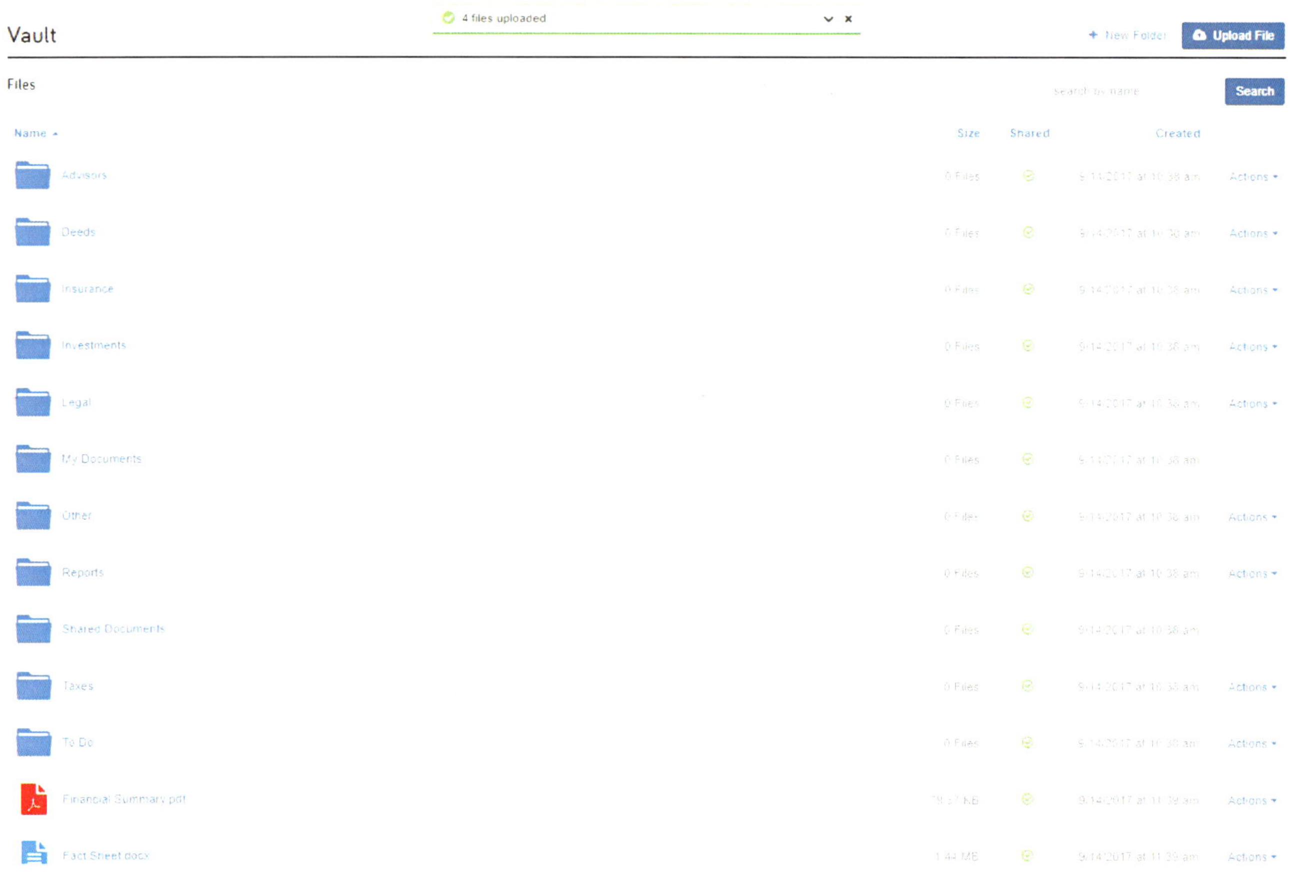

SAFE & SECURE

Your Personal Financial Website employs advanced security features and protocols to keep your data safe, private, and secure at every hour of every day, year round. Our comprehensive security measures include password protection, Secure Socket Layer encryption, firewalls, intrusion detection, audits, inspections, and more.

PEACE OF MIND

With one, centralized and organized location to store all of your important financial documents and files, you and your family will always know where important documents are in times of need.

ACCESS ANYWHERE, ANYTIME

The Vault is accessible from any device so you can review, upload or retrieve your documents from wherever you are.

FILE SHARING OVERSIGHT

Upload files into the Shared Documents folder to make them accessible to your advisor or keep files private and visible to only you by adding them to the My Documents folder.

MINDRIGHT
MONEY MANAGEMENT

VAULT CHECKLIST

Protect Your Important Documents

With unlimited secure document storage, you can organize and protect your most important documents. Review the checklist below and start adding to your Vault today!

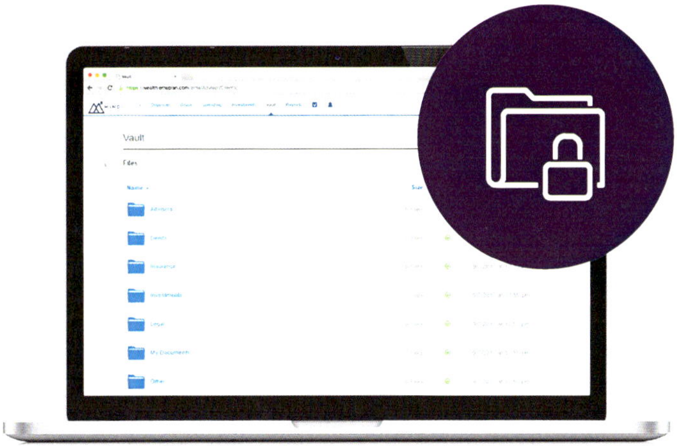

LEGAL DOCUMENTS

- ☐ Wills
- ☐ Deeds
- ☐ Revocable & Irrevocable Trusts
- ☐ Power of Attorney
- ☐ Codicils (Supplements made to a Will)
- ☐ Living Wills/Health Directives
- ☐ Prenuptial Agreements
- ☐ Buy/Sell Agreements
- ☐ Contracts

BENEFITS

- ☐ Social Security Info
- ☐ Veteran's Administration Info
- ☐ Employment Benefits

INSURANCE POLICIES

- ☐ (Life, LTD, Disability, Medical, Car, Property)

BANK & INVESTMENT STATEMENTS

- ☐ Pensions, IRAs, Annuities, etc.
- ☐ Investment Accounts
- ☐ Stock Options/Certificates

LIABILITIES

- ☐ List of Credit Cards with Contact Information
- ☐ Mortgages
- ☐ Loans

TAXES

- ☐ Tax Returns
- ☐ W-2 Forms

IDENTIFICATION

- ☐ Birth Certificates
- ☐ Drivers Licenses
- ☐ Passports
- ☐ Social Security Cards

FAMILY

- ☐ Adoption Papers
- ☐ Medical Records
- ☐ Marriage License
- ☐ Pictures
- ☐ Audio Files
- ☐ Video Clips

PROPERTY

- ☐ Titles to Homes, Autos, Boats, etc.
- ☐ Warranties

MINDRIGHT
MONEY MANAGEMENT

FAQs

Getting Started

CAN THE SITE NOTIFY ME OF MAJOR CHANGES TO MY FINANCIAL ACCOUNTS?

Yes – your Personal Financial Website can alert you via web and email of large deposits, withdrawals, low balances, fees and more. Customize your Alerts by going to ***Settings – Alerts.***

HOW DO I SET UP THE MOBILE WEBSITE?

After you register for your Personal Financial Management website, you will be sent a confirmation email with your username and a link to access the site via your mobile device. Open this email on your mobile device and click on the link. Then click the ***"Add to Home Screen"*** button, or create a mobile bookmark for quick access.

HOW DO I CHANGE MY PASSWORD OR SECURITY QUESTIONS?

Forgotten passwords can be changed by clicking ***Forgot Your Password?*** on your login screen. If you'd like to change your password or security questions, select ***Settings – Security.***

WHAT ARE TASKS?

Tasks are an easy way for your advisor to let you know that something requires your attention in your Personal Financial Website. Tasks work like an online to-do list. Your advisor can assign you a task (such as uploading an important financial document to the Vault before a meeting) and you can instantly notify your advisor once you've completed the request.

WHAT CAN BE UPDATED IN MY SETTINGS?

In the ***Settings*** tab located on the top right of your website, you can make changes to your Alerts, Security, and Privacy settings.

HOW SECURE IS MY FINANCIAL DATA ON THIS SITE?

Your wealth management system employs advanced security features and protocols to keep your data safe, private, and secure at every hour of every day. Our comprehensive security measures include password protection, Secure Socket Layer encryption, firewalls, intrusion detection, audits, inspections, and more. For more information, click ***Security*** in the footer of your website.

HOW CAN I JOIN A SCREEN SHARING SESSION?

To collaborate with your advisor in real time, click the ***Screen Sharing*** link at the bottom right footer and provide your advisor with the session code. If your advisor initiated the session, simply enter the code provided.

The Organizer

HOW DO I ADD MY BANK ACCOUNTS, CREDIT CARDS, AND OTHER FINANCIAL ACCOUNTS TO THIS SYSTEM?

To add your financial accounts, or ***"Connections,"*** follow the steps below:

- On your Client Site homepage, click ***+Add Account*** next to ***Accounts***
- If you have an online login, select ***I have an online login to this account***
- Enter the name of your financial institution into the text box and click ***Search***
- Select the account from the search results and follow the steps to connect

HOW CAN I ADD A PICTURE TO THE PEOPLE AND THINGS IN MY ORGANIZER?

From the Organizer, simply click on the person or thing for which you want to add a picture, and you'll be prompted to upload an image.

Spending & Budgeting

CAN MY WEBSITE CREATE A BUDGET AUTOMATICALLY BASED ON MY SPENDING HABITS?

Yes, you have the option to create your own budget manually or to create an auto-budget using the last 6 months of spending data.

CAN I CHANGE A TRANSACTION THAT IS CLASSIFIED INCORRECTLY?

Our system automatically assigns spending categories to your transactions. If the site has misinterpreted your purchase, you can change the category it's assigned to by navigating to the ***Transactions*** tab under ***Spending.***

Click on the transaction and use the drop down menu to adjust the category.

To change all instances of this transaction type moving forward, create a rule by clicking on the ***Details*** tab underneath the selected transaction. This allows you to rename and reclassify all matching transactions automatically.

CAN MY ADVISOR SEE MY ACCOUNT ACTIVITY?

You have the option of providing your advisor with no spending data, category-only data, or the full view of all data. You can control the privacy of your website under ***Settings – Privacy – Spending Permissions.***

Investments

WHAT TYPE OF INVESTMENT INFORMATION CAN I SEE ON MY WEBSITE?

Your website provides a summary of your entire portfolio as well as a more detailed look into your individual accounts. Account Details include individual holdings, value, asset types, net change in value over time, and transaction history.

CAN I CHANGE MY ASSET ALLOCATION OR CONTRIBUTIONS?

No, for your security, your Personal Financial Management site is non-transactional. Unlike online banking, trading or shopping websites, your money cannot be moved, withdrawn or accessed on our system.

The Vault

HOW DO I ADD A DOCUMENT TO THE VAULT?

To add one or multiple documents to your Vault, simply drag and drop the files from your computer into the desired folder.

WHAT SHOULD I UPLOAD TO MY VAULT?

Your Vault is a secure, easy way to store, organize, and access all your most important documents, like legal documents, medical records, insurance policies, tax information and more. In addition, your advisor can recommend specific documents to upload. To find suggested documents, simply go to the Organizer and click into the fact to view any suggested documents.

MINDRIGHT LEGACY BUILDERS™ FINANCIAL INFORMATION NON-DISCLOSURE

This financial information non-disclosure agreement (the "Agreement") is made between ________________ (the "Disclosing Party") and **MindRight Money Management, LLC** (the "Receiving Party") and is effective ________________. The parties agree as follows:

1. The Transaction

The Agreement is intended to prevent the unauthorized disclosure of Confidential Information (as defined below) in contemplation of a business transaction between the parties (the "Transaction").

2. Confidential Information

Confidential Information" is proprietary information relating to the Transaction including but not limited to: financial institution records, tax records, sales revenues, forecasts, accounting records, investment holdings, wages or income information, or any other financial information that, if disclosed, could affect the Transaction. Confidential information also includes related information that may be disclosed in connection with financial information, including but not limited to identification and account numbers, PINs, passwords, the identity or financial status of investors or partners, or other information conveyed via the **MindRight Legacy Builders™ App**, in writing or in discussion that is indicated to be confidential.

3. Non-Disclosure

Without Disclosing Party's prior written consent, Receiving Party will not: (a) disclose Confidential Information to any third party; (b) make or permit to be made copies or other reproductions of Confidential Information; or (c) make any commercial use of Confidential Information. Receiving Party will carefully restrict access to Confidential Information to those of its officers, directors and employees who are subject to non-disclosure restrictions at least as protective as those set forth in this Agreement and who clearly need such access to participate on Receiving Party's behalf in the analysis and negotiation of a business relationship or any contract or agreement with Disclosing Party.

4. Return of Confidential Materials

Upon Disclosing Party's request, Receiving Party shall within thirty days return all original materials provided by Disclosing Party and any copies, notes or other documents in Receiving Party's possession pertaining to Confidential Information.

5. Term

This Agreement and Receiving Party's duty to hold Confidential Information in confidence shall remain in effect until Disclosing Party sends Receiving Party written notice releasing it from this Agreement.

Disclosing Party:	**Receiving Party:**
____________________________ (Signature)	____________________________ (Signature)
__________________________ (Printed Name)	__________________________ (Printed Name)
Title: ____________________	Title: ____________________
Date: ____________________	Date: ____________________

Made in United States
North Haven, CT
04 November 2026

21736871R00075